Grammar Works
Teacher's Book 2

Mick Gammidge

PUBLISHED BY THE PRESS SYNDICATE OF THE UNIVERSITY OF CAMBRIDGE
The Pitt Building, Trumpington Street, Cambridge CB2 1RP, United Kingdom

CAMBRIDGE UNIVERSITY PRESS
The Edinburgh Building, Cambridge CB2 2RU, United Kingdom
40 West 20th Street, New York, NY 10011–4211, USA
10 Stamford Road, Oakleigh, Melbourne 3166, Australia

© Cambridge University Press 1998

The pages in this book marked 'From **Grammar Works 2** by Mick Gammidge © Cambridge University Press 1998 PHOTOCOPIABLE' may be photocopied free of charge for classroom use by the purchasing individual or institution. this permission to copy does not extend to branches or additional schools of an institution. All other copying is subject to permission from the publisher.

First published 1998

Printed in the United Kingdom at the University Press, Cambridge

ISBN 0 521 62625 0 Teacher's Book 2
ISBN 0 521 55541 8 Student's Book 2

Contents

Unit		Page
	Introduction	1
1	**Are you lazy or hardworking?** review: present simple, *have got*	4
2	**What are they thinking about?** review: present continuous	6
3	**We're going to start a band** review: *going to*	8
4	**Did Columbus find the East?** review: past simple	10
5	**Move slowly and carefully** adverbs of manner	12
6	**Missing meals is bad for you** gerunds	14
	Check point 1 – 6	16
	Double check! 1 – 6	17
7	**Will you go to Mars?** future *will*	18
8	**We shouldn't waste energy** *should*	20
9	**Are you doing anything next Saturday?** present continuous with future meaning; *nobody, something, anywhere*	22
10	**There aren't enough girls** countable and uncountable nouns; *too (much/many), enough, not enough*	24
11	**The biggest in the world!** comparative and superlative adjectives; *as … as, not as … as, … than …*	26
12	**It's the best!** comparative and superlative adjectives with *more* and *most*	28
	Check point 7 – 12	30
	Double check! 7 – 12	31
13	**It was rising from the sea** past continuous affirmative and negative; past simple contrast with *while/when*	32
14	**Which one was driving?** past continuous question forms; *which … ?; one/ones*	34
15	**He is the pilot that built the smallest plane** relative pronouns *who, which, that* in defining relative clauses	36
16	**I really enjoyed myself** reflexive and emphatic pronouns; *each other*	38
17	**I used to forget everything!** *used to* affirmative, negative and question forms	40
18	**I won't be able to live without you** *could/couldn't; will/won't be able to*	42
	Check point 13 – 18	44
	Double check! 13 – 18	45
19	**Smith asked her where the robot was** reported speech	46
20	**You must come home at 10.30** *must; have to; can* for permission	48
21	**The work has been hard** present perfect simple affirmative and negative; *just, already, yet*	50
22	**Where have you put the chocolates?** present perfect simple question forms; *ever … ?*	52
23	**If he isn't fit, he won't play in the big match** first conditional	54
24	**Honey is eaten everywhere** passive – present and past simple	56
	Check point 19 – 24	58
	Double check! 19 – 24	59

Introduction

Grammar Works 2 provides grammar presentation and practice for young students at elementary level. It is suitable for use in class, homework or holiday practice. The grammar syllabus covers those language areas generally taught in second year English courses, and which provide a foundation for further study. *Grammar Works 2* builds on the first 600 vocabulary items used in *Grammar Works 1* and introduces a further 300 words which are recycled throughout the book. The material is flexible and can be used to provide between 28 and 56 hours of study.

Features of *Grammar Works 2*

Grammar Works 2 contains the following features:

- Grammar is presented in context, focusing on both form and meaning.
- An inductive approach encourages students to work out grammar rules for themselves.
- Full grammar tables and explanations for reference are in the Student's Book.
- Explanations are presented in simple language and grammatical terminology is clearly introduced.
- A carefully structured progression through each unit moves from controlled, supportive practice to free practice.
- A range of activity types including inductive exercises, personalisation activities and puzzles provides interest and allows for different learning styles.
- A variety of fun, interesting and educational topics maintains motivation.
- Real world content and (semi-) authentic texts present grammar in a natural and meaningful way.
- Structures and vocabulary are frequently recycled, both within and between units.
- *Check point* units plus an optional photocopiable test assess students' progress every 6 units.
- Optional photocopiable materials for vocabulary practice are provided in the Teacher's Book for each unit.
- The Teacher's Book contains suggestions for further practice activities.

Student's Book

There are 24 teaching units and four *Check point* assessment units in the Student's Book. Each teaching unit has eight exercises, leading the student through a progression of activities as follows:

- Units begin with a grammar presentation through texts which show the grammar point in use and illustrate its meaning. A task accompanies the presentation; this may focus on general comprehension or draw attention to the grammar area but requires no production of the target grammar.

- An inductive exercise follows, focusing students' attention more directly on the form and/or meaning of the grammar just presented. After completing the inductive exercise, students check their ideas in the Grammar reference section at the back of the book. (In a few units where a second grammar point is covered, there is an extra inductive section.)

- The Grammar reference section gives students clearly laid out rules and explanations. While students are encouraged to complete the inductive section before they encounter the Grammar reference section, they can work back and forth if wished.

- The exercises then progress from highly controlled practice, focusing on form but reinforcing meaning, through freer tasks where linguistic support is gradually withdrawn until students are required to produce language in response to contextualising cues.

- Exercise 7 is a personalisation exercise which allows students to use the new grammar to talk about themselves and their world.

- Each unit ends with a puzzle. The puzzle relies on students' understanding of the grammar area covered in the unit but focuses on problem-solving; it thus introduces an element of fun, and encourages the development of general cognitive skills.

- *Check point* units provide a review of the previous six units. Each *Check point* unit has six assessment exercises which are not inductive, nor is there a puzzle.

Teacher's Book

The Teacher's Book contains the following features, corresponding to the student materials:

- Each unit begins with a general description of the grammar point discussing usage, form, pronunciation and potential difficulties for students, as appropriate.
- All the new vocabulary for the unit is listed.
- Answers to exercises and puzzles are given (including answers to photocopiable worksheets in the Teacher's Book).

- Suggestions are given for supplementary practice activities based around pairwork, groupwork and classwork with advice on how and when to use these. They are generally more communicative activities than the written exercises in the Student's Book.
- For each of the teaching units, there is a page of photocopiable vocabulary practice. This worksheet can be used for presentation, practice and written record of new words in the unit. Where appropriate, vocabulary sets are extended a little from the Student's Book in these worksheets.
- For each *Check point* unit in the Student's Book, there is a photocopiable worksheet (*Double check!*), which provides further assessment material for the previous six units.

Using the Student's Book

Presentation texts

All units begin with an illustrated text which clearly presents the form and the meaning of the new grammar area. It is a good idea to preview the contexts, and in some units specific suggestions are given. You could use various approaches to preview the context, possibly using mother tongue, for example:

- Ask students what they already know about the general topic area before they see the text.
- Students look at the illustrations in the context and name as many items as they can in English.
- Students look at the type of text in the context and identify its source, e.g. newspaper, text book, comic, etc.
- In some units, the photocopiable worksheets can be used with the preview activity to preteach necessary vocabulary. The new vocabulary can be presented via the illustrations in the worksheet activities, which can then be completed for practice.

Inductive exercises

Although answers to inductive exercises are provided at the back of the Student's Book, students should be encouraged to see these exercises as a challenge where they work out rules for themselves before checking their ideas at the back of the book. By checking their answers and studying any additional information, students can be sure they are on the right track before proceeding to the main body of exercises for which answers are given only in the Teacher's Book.

Other exercises

More mechanical question and answer exercises can provide useful, confidence-building drill practice where students ask and answer each other in pairs. Pairwork can be used as a general strategy both to extend communication, and to allow students to compare their ideas and thus become more reflective about their learning. You might remind students that they can learn from each other.

Personalisation exercises

Personalisation exercises in each unit give students the opportunity to relate the language to their own world and experience. Students' answers will vary and can be used as the basis for a range of follow-up activities, for example:

- Students compare the content of their answers with a partner.
- Students report either their own or their partner's answers back to the class.
- Students take part in class surveys.

Puzzles

The puzzle is intended to be a fun activity and students should not worry if they can't work out the correct answer. You might want to put students in co-operative groups, or set a time limit for solving the puzzle. You could conduct the puzzle as a race between groups. Some puzzles could be used as a model for students to write similar puzzles if they enjoy this kind of activity.

Supplementing the Student's Book

Grammar Works 2 provides essential grammar presentation and practice focusing on both form and meaning. Grammar terminology is introduced gradually from the beginning, and you may wish to ensure that students learn the most important terms as they go along. You can supplement the material in the Student's Book with suggestions in the Teacher's Book and your own ideas to work on other aspects of language and language use to help develop overall communicative competence. Other areas to consider include:

Vocabulary

A good vocabulary provides students with the basic building blocks which, along with grammar, allow them to understand and express ideas in English. Most of the vocabulary in *Grammar Works 2* is introduced in a way which makes its meaning clear, and there are photocopiable, supplementary vocabulary worksheets for each unit in the Teacher's Book. You may wish to extend the vocabulary beyond the 300 or so words presented. There are various ways of doing this, for example:

- Use the illustrations in the Student's Book to teach items which are not named in the materials.
- Supplement the word sets in the contexts with other related, common, key vocabulary.
- Where members of common word sets, e.g. colours, numbers, days of the week, food, occur in the materials, use these as an opportunity to recycle or teach other members.

- Where words have common antonyms or synonyms appropriate to your students' level, you could introduce these.

Reading

The Student's Book contains reading materials in various forms. The contexts include a variety of text types, e.g. advertisements, magazine articles, text books, comic strips, film review, dialogues, many of which are adapted from authentic sources. You can exploit these texts to develop reading subskills: guessing vocabulary from context; identifying text type; skimming (reading for general topic or gist) by asking broad questions before the students read, e.g. *What is it about?*; scanning (reading for obvious details such as numbers, dates, etc.).

For skimming and scanning, students should be given only a short time to read. They can then read the text again more slowly for fuller understanding, which you could check by devising comprehension questions.

Some of the units contain cloze exercises which develop reading skills related to cohesion/coherence.

The puzzles also usually provide short but intensive texts for reading practice. If students find it difficult to solve a puzzle, you could ask them to translate it into their own language to check detailed comprehension.

Writing

Within each unit, support is gradually withdrawn so that in personalisation exercises, students are required to generate their own complete sentences.

There are some specific suggestions for additional writing activities in the Teacher's Book. You can use group project and poster work in particular to encourage students to produce written sentences on subjects that you know interest them. These can be ongoing and continuously extended.

Speaking

Pairwork and groupwork will maximise students' opportunity to practise their spoken English. The Teacher's Book gives guidance on pronunciation features specific to the grammar areas considered. Encourage students to use contracted forms when they speak.

For freer group activities like project work, encourage students to use as much English as they can during the process. You can offer language support but you don't need to be overly concerned about accuracy (or mother tongue use), as this is a chance for students to take risks and develop fluency and confidence; the product (for example, the poster) will provide the accuracy focus. You can also teach students useful classroom language, *How do I say … in English? What does … mean?* etc.

Listening

Listening, like speaking, is an inevitable part of communicative pairwork and groupwork, e.g. *Find someone who …* activities. In more routine interactions, such as comparing answers to exercises, the emphasis can be placed on listening by asking students to do these orally without looking at their partner's answers.

You can also devise short dictation exercises, recycling the grammar and vocabulary students have learnt so far.

Conclusion

Grammar Works 2 attempts to make the study of English grammar a meaningful and fun experience for young students. It also aims to make grammar teaching varied, innovative and interesting, and I hope that both you and your students enjoy using the materials.

Mick Gammidge

1 Are you lazy or hardworking?

Review: present simple
Conjunctions *and, or, but, so*

Although the main focus of this unit is the present simple and conjunctions, students are required to produce earlier areas of the grammar syllabus, e.g. *be, can, have got.*

Present simple: Meaning
Present simple here refers to general time, rather than the specific present moment, and represents ongoing states or repeated actions.

Form
- Students may forget that *she/he/it* take a different form of the verb in the present simple, e.g. *I know/he knows, I don't know/he doesn't know.*
- Spelling rules for 3rd person *-s* are the same as plural *-s* for nouns.
  – verbs ending in *-ch, -o, -sh, -s, -x or -z*: add *-es*
  – verbs ending in *-y*: remove *-y* and add *-ies*
  – other verbs: add *-s*
- The auxiliary verb *do/does* is not usually used in affirmatives and may cause problems for students. They may either include *do/does* in the affirmative (which is only used for strong emphasis or contradiction), or omit *do/does* in the negative: **I do live ... *I no live ...*I not live ...*
- Questions in the present simple are made by putting the auxiliary *do/does* before the subject. The main verb does not move and is in the infinitive without *to*. Question words (*who, what*, etc.) are placed at the beginning of questions before the auxiliary verb.
- The negative is usually contracted in spoken and written English except for emphasis or in formal situations.

Pronunciation
Pronunciation of the auxiliary *do* in question forms is /də/. In spoken English, *do you* is often pronounced /djuː/. In short answers, *do* as the final word is pronounced fully, /duː/, and is stressed.

Conjunctions: *and, or, but, so*
These conjunctions are introduced in *Grammar Works 1* where students are required to understand them but not produce them. In this unit, students are required to distinguish between them and use them to link sentences.

Vocabulary
Nouns: *farm, hamster, rabbit*
Verb: *teach*

▶ **Worksheet A, B, C, D**

Preview activity
Draw students' attention to *English* and *letter*. Ask *Who do you write letters to?* and *Who do you write letters to in English?* Elicit *pen friend* and ask students *Have you got any pen friends?* as a lead-in to the presentation text, i.e. Sue's letter to her pen friend.

Student's Book answers
1 1 Kim 2 Sue 3 James 4 Paulo
2 1 and 2 but 3 or 4 so
3a + I **play** an instrument.
       She **plays** an instrument.
   – I **don't play** an instrument.
       She **doesn't play** an instrument.
   ? **Do** you **play** an instrument?
       Does she **play** an instrument?

b 1 loves 2 studies 3 watches 4 plays
c 1 teaches 2 carries 3 stays 4 likes
4 1 Are you lazy or hardworking?
   2 He hasn't got a bike, so he walks to school.
   3 Is it raining or (is it) snowing?
   4 He's got a broken leg, so he can't play football.
   5 I'm small but (I'm) strong.
   6 She studies music and (she) plays the piano.

▶ **Worksheet E**

Student's Book answers
5 1 is 2 am 3 live 4 keep 5 've (have) got
   6 watch 7 write 8 love 9 don't like 10 hate
6 1 What is her name? 2 How old is she? 3 Where does she live? 4 What does she do in her free time?
   5 Does she like animals? 6 How many pets has she got?
   7 Does she like homework?

Pairwork suggestion
Students ask each other questions 2–7, *How old are you? Where do you live?* etc. Then partners report back to the class, using 3rd person present simple with *she/he*.

Student's Book answers
7 Answers will vary.

Classwork suggestion
Ask students to remove their name from their letters. Collect the letters and distribute them randomly. Students ask each other questions based on the contents of the letters to identify the writer.

Student's Book answers

Puzzle
Four – on the return journey, the bus is on the opposite side of the road, so if Tim is now looking on his right (rather than on his left on the way to school), he is counting the same pet shops.

Worksheet

Extra vocabulary: *calculator*

Use A, B, C, and D before the preview activity to review the vocabulary for the context.

A Answers will vary according to students' first language.
B 1 telescope 2 drums 3 guitar 4 football 5 letter
6 calculator
C 1 telescope = science; 2 drums = music; 3 guitar = music;
4 football = sports; 5 letter = English; 6 calculator = maths
D 1 history 2 French
E Use this activity to revise verbs as preparation for exercise 5.

Answers
1 love 2 keep 3 carry 4 play 5 stay 6 study 7 teach
8 watch
a watch b play c study d teach e keep f carry
g love h stay

Are you lazy or hardworking? Worksheet 1

A Look at the school timetable. Write the names of the school subjects in your language.

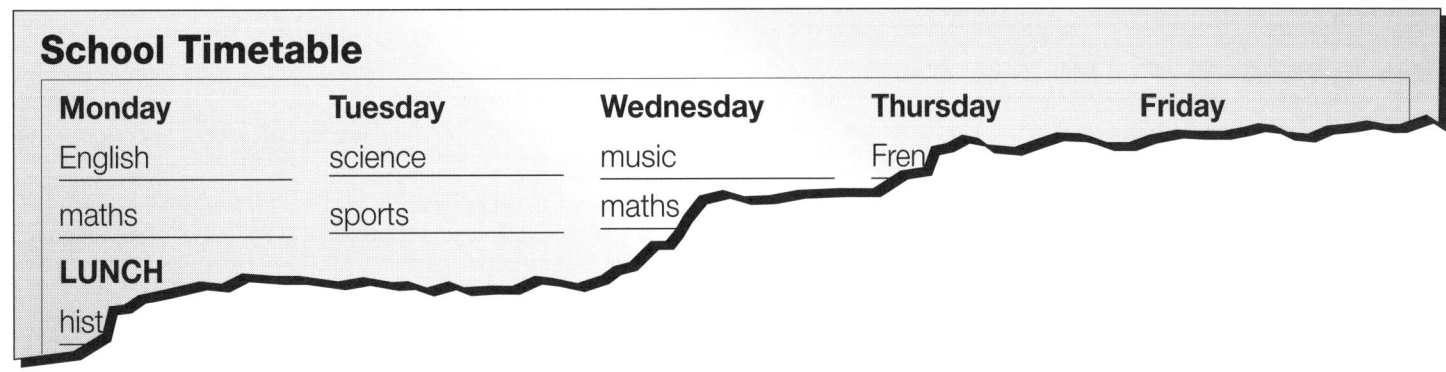

B Now look at the pictures and write the words below with the correct pictures.

calculator   drums   football   guitar   letter   ~~telescope~~

1 telescope   2 _____   3 _____   4 _____   5 _____   6 _____

C Match the pictures in activity B with the school subjects.

1 science   2 _____   3 _____   4 _____   5 _____   6 _____

D Can you complete these subjects on the timetable? (You can use your dictionary.)

1 his_____   2 Fren_____

E Put the letters in the correct order and make verbs. Then complete the sentences below with the verbs.

1 v o l e | l | o | v | e |
2 p e k e
3 c r y r a
4 y a l p

5 y a s t
6 d u t s y
7 c a t h e
8 c w a t h

a We _____ programmes on TV.
b I _____ football.
c You _____ English at school.
d Our teachers _____ us English.

e Farmers _____ animals.
f I _____ books in my school bag.
g Rabbits __love__ eating carrots.
h I _____ up late at weekends.

From **GRAMMAR WORKS 2** by Mick Gammidge
© Cambridge University Press 1998

2 What are they thinking about?

Review: present continuous

Meaning
The present continuous with the function of action in progress now and around now is contrasted here with the present simple. (See Unit 1.) Verbs that denote a state/condition (e.g. *be, love, like, know*) generally take a simple tense. Similarly, verbs of sense, (e.g. *smell, see, taste, hear*) also generally use *can* rather than the continuous form except where they denote deliberate actions.

Form
- The present continuous is formed using the auxiliary verb *be* and the *-ing* form of the verb.
- Questions in the present continuous are made by putting the auxiliary *am/is/are* before the subject. The *-ing* form of the main verb does not move. Short answers drop the main verb and end with the auxiliary.
- Question words (*who, what*, etc.) are placed at the beginning of questions before the auxiliary verb.
- The negative is usually contracted in spoken and written English except for emphasis or in formal situations.
- Spelling rules for *-ing* forms are as follows:
  – For verbs ending in more than one consonant or ending in more than one vowel and then one consonant, add *-ing*, e.g. *watching, cooking*.
  – Verbs ending in one vowel and one consonant, double the consonant and add *-ing*, e.g. *swimming*. Note that verbs ending in the consonants *-w, -y* or *-x* do not follow this rule and these consonants do not double. With verbs of more than one syllable this rule becomes more complex. When the stress is on the last syllable, the final consonant doubles, e.g. *beginning*. Where the stress is not on the final syllable, then the final consonant is not doubled, e.g. *listening*. However, there are some irregular verbs that do not follow these rules, e.g. *travelling*.
  – Verbs ending in *-e* drop the *-e* and add *-ing*, e.g. *making*.
  – Verbs ending in *-ie*, change *-ie* to *-y* and add *-ing*.

Vocabulary
Verbs: *begin, chase, cry, happen, look at, wave, work*
Nouns: *artist, food, painter, painting, passenger, ship*
Adverb: *away*

Preview activity
Elicit or preteach *to paint* and *a painting* (noun). Ask students *Do you paint/like painting?* Ask students what paintings/painters they know. Note that although the picture is obviously in the past, the present continuous is generally used to describe all pictures as though they are happening now.

Student's Book answers
1b Example answers
  1 I think that/I don't think that the ship is sailing away.
  2 I think that/I don't think that they are beginning a new life.
2a 1 They are sitting on a ship.
  2 They aren't looking.
  3 Is the ship sailing away?
  4 What are they thinking?
  b 1 She is holding her baby's hand.
  2 The man and woman aren't looking.
  3 Is the baby sleeping?
  4 Where are they going?

3a 1 looking 2 coming 3 lying 4 sitting
  b 1 driving 2 dying 3 jumping 4 running
4 1 She's eating a sandwich.
  2 They aren't listening to the teacher.
  3 It isn't lying down.
  4 She's taking a photo.
  5 They're walking on the grass.

▶ *Worksheet*

Student's Book answers
5 1 are … doing 2 'm painting 3 's walking 4 Is … crying
  5 she isn't/she's not … , 's shouting 6 is … shouting
  7 are running 8 're chasing 9 's looking

Writing suggestion
Bring pictures of paintings or photos to class. Students write descriptions and give their opinions using the present continuous and *think that …* .

Student's Book answers
6 1 is 2 isn't working 3 's taking 4 's visiting 5 enjoys
  6 's sitting 7 (is) drawing 8 are playing 9 is watching
7 Answers will vary.
  1 Yes, I do./No, I don't. 2 Yes, I am./No, I'm not.
  3 I'm wearing … 4 Yes, I do./No, I don't.
  5 I'm … ing …

Groupwork suggestion
Write different jobs on slips of paper and give a separate slip to each member of the group. Each member of the group mimes an action associated with the job on their piece of paper. The other students can ask two yes/no questions, one with the present continuous, the other with *be*, e.g. *Are you making an omelette? Are you a cook?* Points are scored for *yes* answers and when the two questions are correctly asked, another member of the group mimes their job.

Extension activity
Groups think of a new job with associated actions. Then the most confident member of each group (or the winner) mimes the job to the class. The competition is repeated between groups.

Student's Book answers

Puzzle
Three – from left to right – girl, girl, boy.

Worksheet

Use these activities before exercise 5 to preteach *chase, cry, look for* and to practise the verbs in the unit. After students finish activity A, elicit the fact that the answers are in alphabetical order and provide a verb picture dictionary for reference. Activity B practises spelling rules for the *-ing* form.

Answers
A 1 chase 2 cry 3 draw 4 drive 5 eat 6 lie 7 listen
  8 look for 9 paint 10 run 11 sail 12 shout 13 sit
  14 think 15 wave 16 work
B 1 crying 2 sailing 3 eating 4 chasing 5 listening
  6 looking 7 driving 8 painting 9 drawing 10 thinking
  11 lying 12 running 13 shouting 14 waving 15 sitting
  16 working

What are they thinking about? Worksheet 2

A Write the verbs below with the pictures.

wave   sail   sit   think   drive   lie   run   eat   listen   paint   cry   shout   chase   look for   work   draw

1 _____

2 _____

3 _____

4 _____

5 _____

6 _____

7 _____

8 _____

9 _____

10 _____

11 _____

12 _____

13 _____

14 _____

15 _____

16 _____

B Now use the verbs to complete the sentences.

1 Her little brother is sad. He's _____ing.

2 The ship is _____ing on the sea.

3 She's _____ing a burger.

4 The dog is _____ing the cat.

5 They're _____ing to music.

6 He's _____ing for a book in the bookshop.

7 She's _____ing a car.

8 He's _____ing his house white.

9 She's _____ing a picture.

10 The students are _____ing about the answer.

11 He's _____ing in bed.

12 She's late, so she's _____ing.

13 He's angry, so he's _____ing.

14 They're _____ing to their friends.

15 She's _____ing on a chair.

16 We're not on holiday. We're _____ing.

From GRAMMAR WORKS 2 by Mick Gammidge
© Cambridge University Press 1998

PHOTOCOPIABLE

3 We're going to start a band

Review: be + going to + verb; + and – forms

Meaning
Going to is a common future form in English, and has many uses. This unit revises *going to* for talking about intentions. Other common uses, as presented in *Grammar Works 1*, are:
- saying that something is about to happen, either intentionally or accidentally, based on present evidence. Often we can see the action actually starting.
- making general predictions.

Form
- The construction uses the auxiliary verb *be* plus *going to* plus the infinitive of the main verb without *to*.
- The auxiliary *be* is generally contracted in spoken English except for emphasis or in formal contexts. In written English, the full form is generally used except in informal situations.

Pronunciation
The pronunciation of *to* in *going* is generally /tə/.

Vocabulary
Verbs: *argue, bite, buy, cut, dye, forget, get*
Nouns: *art, band, biology, fingernail, interpreter, junk food, literature, musician, New Year, physics, present, resolution*
Adjective: *healthy*

Preview activity
Elicit or preteach *band* (and the synonym *pop group*). Ask students *Do you like music? What bands/groups do you like? Do you play an instrument? What instruments do you play?*

Student's Book answers
1b 1 No, she doesn't. 2 No, she isn't.
2 + She**'s going to** get a present.   They**'re going to** buy new clothes.
   – She**'s not** / She **isn't going to** dye her hair.   He**'s not** / He **isn't going to** start piano lessons.
   ? **Is** she **going to** dye her hair?   **Are** they **going to** start a band?
3 1 Ann's going to be a doctor.
   2 Ben's going to be an artist.
   3 Liz's going to be an interpreter.
   4 Abdul and Sue are going to be scientists.
   5 Tansy's going to be a musician.
   6 Tim's going to be a writer.
4 **Example answers**
   1 Ann's going to study biology. She's not going to study music.
   2 Ben's going to study art. He's not going to study biology.
   3 Liz's going to study French. She's not going to study music.
   4 Abdul and Sue are going to study physics. They're not going to study French.
   5 Tansy's going to study music. She's not going to study art.

▶ *Worksheet*

Pairwork suggestion
Students ask each other their plans for study and/or jobs. Then they report to the class.

Student's Book answers
5 1 Is Sue going to get a present?
   2 What is Sue going to learn?
   3 What are Kim and Sue going to start?
   4 What are they going to buy?
   5 Is Sue going to dye her hair?

6 1 are you doing 2 'm writing 3 is 4 argue 5 'm going to stop 6 'm not going to bite 7 'm going to practise 8 Have … got 9 eat 10 'm going to eat 11 'm going to do 12 'm not going to forget 13 is
7 Answers will vary.

Classwork activity
Students ask each other questions to find someone who has the same resolution as themselves. When they have found a partner, they sit down.

Student's Book answers

Puzzle

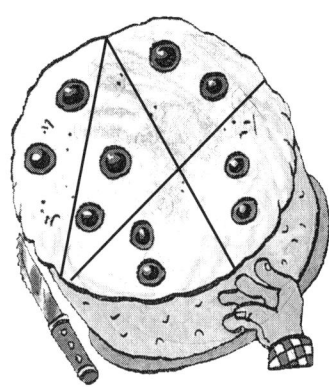

Worksheet

Use these activities after exercise 4 to review jobs vocabulary and other words which can be associated with the jobs.

Answers
A 1 actor 2 artist 3 dentist 4 doctor 5 farmer 6 interpreter 7 musician 8 painter 9 scientist 10 singer 11 teacher 12 writer
B a film b headache c languages d music e paint f picture g school h science i songs j story k teeth l vegetables
C a actor b doctor c interpreter d musician e painter f artist g teacher h scientist i singer j writer k dentist l farmer

Groupwork extension activities
1 Students make a list of other words they know which relate to the jobs here.
2 Students think of other jobs and related words.
3 Students decide which school subjects are important for the jobs.

We're going to start a band

Worksheet 3

A Complete the words for the jobs in the pictures below.

1 a c t o r
2 a _ _ _ _ _
3 d _ _ _ _ _
4 d _ _ _ _
5 f _ _ _ _ _
6 i _ _ _ _ _ _ _ _ _

7 m _ _ _ _ _ _ _
8 p _ _ _ _ _
9 s _ _ _ _ _ _ _
10 s _ _ _ _ _
11 t _ _ _ _ _ _
12 w _ _ _ _ _

B Complete the words for the things in the pictures below.

a f i l m
b h _ a _ a _ h
c l _ n _ u _ g _ s
d m _ s _ c
e p _ i _ t
f p _ c _ u _ e
g s _ h _ o _
h s _ i _ n _ e
i s _ n _ s
j s _ o _ y
k t _ e _ h
l v _ g _ t _ b _ e _

C Now match each thing in activity B with a job from activity A.

a actor
b _____
c _____
d _____
e _____
f _____
g _____
h _____
i _____
j _____
k _____
l _____

From **GRAMMAR WORKS 2** by Mick Gammidge
© Cambridge University Press 1998

4 Did Columbus find the East?

Review: past simple

Meaning
You may wish to remind students that the past simple is used for states or actions in the past.

Form
- In negatives, where *do/does/don't/doesn't* is used in the present simple, *did/didn't* is used in the past simple and the main verb remains in the infinitive.
- **Spelling rules** for past simple forms:
  Words ending in:
  - -y: -y + -ie + -ed   stud**ied**, carr**ied**
  - -e: + -d   like**d**, love**d**
  - a vowel and then a consonant (for example: *-ir, -op, -ip*): double the consonant + -ed   sti**rred**, sto**pped**

Note that verbs ending in the consonants *-w, -y* or *-x* do not follow this rule and these consonants do not double, e.g. *showed, played, fixed.*
  - Other words: + -ed   start**ed**, look**ed**, watch**ed**

Pronunciation
Pronunciation of past simple regular verb endings depends on the final sound of the verb.
- When the final sound is /t/ or /d/ the ending *-ed* is pronounced /ɪd/.
- When the final sound is voiced, /b, g, v, ʒ, z, dʒ, m, l, n, ŋ/, or a vowel sound, the ending is pronounced /d/.
- When the final sound is unvoiced, /k, f, p, tʃ, s, ʃ/, the ending is pronounced /t/.
- Verbs with irregular past forms simply have to be learnt – there is no general guiding rule to predict the past form from the infinitive.

Vocabulary
Verbs: *agree, believe, build, travel*
Nouns: *bone, corn, Earth, guide book, money, museum, shell, Spain, sweet, sweet potato, tool, town, wood*
Adjective: *round*

▶ **Worksheet**

Preview activity
Ask students to cover the text in exercise 1 and look at the picture. Ask them *What can you see in the picture? What is happening in the picture? What year do you think it is? Where do you think it is? Who do you think the people are?* Students then read the text to check their answers.

Student's Book answers
1 1 moved – move   2 lived – live   3 made – make
    4 read – read   5 knew – know   6 thought – think
    7 sailed – sail   8 asked – ask   9 agreed – agree
    10 found – find

2a + He **lived** in Lisbon.
    – The Portuguese **didn't believe** him.
    ? **Did** Columbus **find** the East?
       Why **did** he **take** Spanish ships?
b + He found South America.
    – He didn't sail East.
    ? Did he sail West?
       Where did he live?

3 1 visited   2 He went   3 They travelled   4 They saw
    5 They left   6 James/He enjoyed

4 1 James didn't go to the restaurant.
    2 James didn't buy a guide book.
    3 James read the information.
    4 James watched a video.
    5 James didn't see the dinosaurs.

5 1 What did you visit?
    2 Who did you go with?
    3 How did you travel?
    4 What did you see?
    5 When did you leave?
    6 Did you enjoy your day?

6 1 found   2 lived   3 made   4 fished   5 met   6 didn't speak
    7 didn't speak   8 were   9 gave   10 gave   11 were
    12 grew   13 made   14 built   15 lived   16 are   17 live
    18 speak

Project work activity
Students write a short account, or make a poster with pictures, about an explorer famous in their country.

Student's Book answers
7 Answers will vary.

Pairwork activity
Students ask their partner questions like those in exercise 5 to find out about their last visit. Then pairs report to the class about their partner.

Student's Book answers

Puzzle
A clock/watch. To say a watch 'doesn't go' means it's broken.

Worksheet
Use these activities before the preview activity to preteach and revise vocabulary necessary for this unit.

Answers
A 1 ask   2 answer   3 think   4 agree   5 understand   6 argue
    7 believe

B 1 ship   2 sea   3 wood   4 stone   5 bone   6 shell   7 bottle
    8 fish   9 boat   10 telescope   11 map   12 beach

Did Columbus find the East?

Worksheet 4

A Write the words below with the correct pictures.

agree   answer   argue   ~~ask~~   believe   think   understand

1. ask
2. _____
3. _____
4. _____
5. _____
6. _____
7. _____

B Put the letters in the correct order and make words for the things in the picture. Then match the things in the picture with the words.

1. pish — ship
2. ase _____
3. dowo _____
4. etons _____
5. beno _____
6. slehl _____
7. telbot _____
8. hifs _____
9. atob _____
10. poscelete _____
11. pam _____
12. chabe _____

From GRAMMAR WORKS 2 by Mick Gammidge
© Cambridge University Press 1998

PHOTOCOPIABLE

5 Move slowly and carefully

Adverbs of manner

Meaning
Here adverbs are used to describe verbs.

Form
- Spelling rules for adverbs:
  When an adjective ends in:
  - *-y* drop *-y* and add *-ily*. busy – busily
  - consonant + *-le* drop *-e* and add *-y* simple – simply, comfortable – comfortably
  - All other adjectives + *-ly* brave – bravely, careful – carefully, bad – badly
- There are some irregular adverbs. For example: *good – well hard – hard fast – fast high – high.*
- It may also be a good idea to point out to students that not all words ending in *-ly* are adverbs, for example *silly*.
- Note that in this unit verbs are used without objects. When verbs are used with objects, the adverb follows the object, for example *He plays well. / He plays the piano well.*

Vocabulary
Nouns: *cheetah, day, eagle, eater, monkey, night, owl, rider, snake, tortoise, worker*
Adjectives: *careful, comfortable, easy, gentle, hard, loud, noisy, patient, quiet, silent, simple, strange*
Adverbs: *badly, bravely, busily, carefully, comfortably, dangerously, easily, gently, happily, loudly, noisily, patiently, quietly, silently, simply, slowly, specially, terribly, well*

▶ **Worksheet A**

Preview activity
Ask students *Do you like animals? What animals do you like? Have you got any pets? What pets have you got? Do you like wild animals? Do you like watching wild animals?* Then look at the picture with the presentation text and preteach *owl*. Ask students what they know about owls. Ask *Can owls see/hear/run/fly? Do they fly at night or in the day? Do they hunt?* Students then read the text to check their answers.

Student's Book answers
1 1 yes 2 yes 3 no

2
Adjectives	Adverbs
careful	carefully
comfortable	comfortably
easy	easily
fast	fast
good	well
patient	patiently
quiet	quietly
silent	silently
slow	slowly

3 1 bus**y** – bus**ily** happ**y** – happ**ily**
2 dangerous – dangerous**ly** brave – brave**ly**
3 beautiful – beautiful**ly** special – special**ly**
4 sim**ple** – sim**ply** gen**tle** – gen**tly**

Classwork suggestion
Write a list of adverbs, adjectives and words which are adjectives and adverbs (e.g. *fast*) on the board. Students copy these, sort them under the correct one of the three headings *adverbs, adjectives, adjectives and adverbs*. You could include opposites which students additionally match.

Student's Book answers
4a fast – fast good – well high – high noisy – noisily
silent – silently slow – slowly
b 1 Cheetahs run fast.
2 Eagles fly high.
3 Tortoises walk slowly.
4 Pigs eat noisily.
5 Snakes move silently.
6 Monkeys climb well.

▶ **Worksheet B**

Student's Book answers
5 1 She drives carefully. 6 She rides fast.
2 He painted badly. 7 He works hard.
3 They sing loudly. 8 She writes terribly.
4 He acted well. 9 He cooks excellently.
5 They eat noisily.
6 1 dangerously 2 hard 3 easily 4 patiently 5 loudly
6 quietly 7 fast 8 slowly

Classwork activities
- You can play a version of 'Simple Simon says …' where you tell students to respond only if you put *Simple Simon says* before your command and you give instructions including adverbs, e.g. *Walk slowly, Simple Simon says sit down quickly.* Students are out of the game if they do the action wrongly or if they do it when you haven't said *Simple Simon says* first. You can ask a student to lead the class in the game once they have understood how the game works.
- Alternatively, ask students to write a verb + adverb combination on a slip of paper, e.g. *drive carefully*. Collect all the slips and hand them out to students. Tell students not to show their papers to anyone. Students mime the activity and the class guess what is written on the paper.

Student's Book answers
7 Answers will vary.

Extension activity
For 3rd person practice, students write five more sentences about the talents of their friends or members of their family.

Student's Book answers

Puzzle
quietly – the first letter of the adverb is the next in the alphabet to the first letter of the verb.

Worksheet

A Use this activity before the preview activity to preteach and revise some adjectives used in this unit.

Answers
1 b 2 a 3 a 4 a 5 a 6 a 7 b 8 a 9 a

B Use this activity after exercise 4 to review animal names. You can ask students to cover the word list at the top of the activity and see how many words (including correct spellings) they can remember before they look at the list for help.

Answers
1 an owl 2 a leopard 3 a rabbit 4 an eagle 5 a cheetah
6 a monkey 7 a tortoise 8 a snake 9 hamster

Move slowly and carefully

Worksheet 5

A Tick (✓) the correct picture for each word.

1 a ____ careful b ✓	2 a ____ comfortable b ____	3 a ____ easy b ____
4 a ____ gentle b ____	5 a ____ high b ____	6 a ____ loud b ____
7 a ____ noisy b ____	8 a ____ patient b ____	9 a ____ simple b ____

B Complete these sentences about a holiday in Africa.
Use *a* or *an* and the words below.

cheetah   eagle   hamster   leopard   monkey   ~~owl~~   rabbit   snake   tortoise

1 This is _an_ _owl_ .

2 This is ____ ____ .

3 This is ____ ____ .

4 This is ____ ____ .

5 This is ____ ____ .

6 This is ____ ____ .

7 This is ____ ____ .

8 This is ____ ____ .

9 And this is Fred, my pet

____ ____ . He came too!

6 Missing meals is bad for you

Gerunds
- The gerund is introduced here as subject and reviewed as object.
- *Not* is placed before the gerund to make negatives. Here the gerund phrases are kept short, e.g. <u>Not cooking with oil</u> *is good*. – but they can be quite long e.g. <u>Going out in winter without a coat on</u> *is bad*.
- Remind students that the spelling rules for the gerund are the same as the rules for making the *-ing* form of the present continuous.
- *Go* + gerund is often used for leisure activities (but not team games), e.g. *go camping, go climbing, go cycling, go diving, go fishing, go jogging, go sailing, go sightseeing, go shopping*
- *Let's go* + gerund is used to make suggestions for 1st person plural groups. In modern English, the full form *Let us* is almost never used.

Vocabulary
Verbs: *camp, cycle, dive, exercise, smoke*
Nouns: *countryside, hobby, idea, leisure activities, jogging, meal, sightseeing*
Adjectives: *boring, difficult, fun, important*
Adverb: *regularly*

Preview activity
Introduce the topic of the unit by asking students *What food do you like? What do you eat every day? Is (that food) good for you / bad for you? What other things are good for you / bad for you?*

Student's Book answers
1 1 good   2 bad   3 good
2a 1 living   2 Missing   3 Not cooking
 b 1 The book is about eating healthy food.
   2 Eating healthy food is good for you.
   3 Not eating healthy food is bad for you.
3 driving going lying staying learning swimming
   1 swimming 2 Driving 3 playing 4 lying 5 Staying
   6 Going
4 1 Not cooking 2 Smoking 3 Not eating 4 Not drinking
   5 Not exercising 6 Not eating 7 Eating 8 Not sleeping
5a Let's **go** swim**ming**.
 b 1 Sue went swimming last week.
   2 Sue isn't going swimming.
   3 Does Sue go swimming every week?
   4 Sue didn't go swimming yesterday.
6 1 went swimming 2 go shopping 3 go jogging
   4 go cycling 5 went camping

Groupwork suggestion
In threes, students practise the following drill:
S1: *I like/love (going)* gerund e.g. *I like going swimming.*
S2: *She/He thinks that* gerund *is* adjective. e.g. *She thinks that going swimming is healthy.*
S3: *Let's ...* e.g. *Let's go swimming / to the pool.*

Student's Book answers
7 Answers will vary.

Class activity
Students move around the class trying to find someone with the same opinion as them. They ask questions based on their answers, e.g. *Do you think that camping is fun/boring?* When they find someone with the same opinion, they sit down.

Student's Book answers
Puzzle
Eric = swimming   James = cycling   Sue = swimming
Kim = shopping – by a process of elimination.

▶ *Worksheet*

Worksheet
Extra vocabulary: *skating, windsurfing*

Use this activity at the end of the unit to review gerunds which are common outdoor activities. Tell students not to look at the words at the bottom of the page unless they need to.

Answers
1 walking 2 jogging 3 camping 4 climbing 5 sightseeing
6 painting 7 riding 8 cycling 9 skating 10 swimming
11 diving 12 fishing 13 sailing 14 water-skiing
15 windsurfing

Missing meals is bad for you

Worksheet 6

Read the holiday brochure and write the names of the activities. (You can look at the words at the bottom of the page for help.)

At Sunny Park you can go:

SUNNY PARK

1. walking
2.
3.
4.
5.
6.
7.
8.
9.
10.
11.
12.
13.
14.
15.

camping climbing cycling diving fishing horseriding jogging painting riding sailing sightseeing skating swimming ~~walking~~ water-skiing windsurfing

From GRAMMAR WORKS 2 by Mick Gammidge
© Cambridge University Press 1998

PHOTOCOPIABLE

15

Check point 1-6

1a 1 When do you get up?
2 What do you eat for breakfast?
3 What do you like doing?
4 What instrument do you play?
5 Have you got a girlfriend?
b Answers will vary.
2 1 are 2 is playing 3 wins 4 are arguing 5 agree
6 is watching 7 isn't enjoying 8 doesn't like
9 loves 10 are … doing
3 1 It's raining, so she's going to wear her hat.
2 He's studying French because he's going to go to France on holiday.
3 They're going to a café because they're going to have lunch.
4 It's snowing, so she's going to stay at home.
4a 1 Who was 2 When did 3 Who was 4 Where did
b 1 was 2 lived 3 taught 4 went 5 visited 6 didn't go
7 stopped 8 didn't have 9 died
c 1 King Philip of Macedon 2 365 to 323 BC 3 Aristotle 4 India
5

Adjectives	Adverbs
dangerous – careful	dangerously – carefully
good – bad	well – badly
slow – fast	slowly – fast
quiet – noisy/loud	quietly – noisily/loudly

6 1 He drives dangerously. His driving is dangerous.
2 She cooks well. Her cooking is good.
3 She sings loudly. Her singing is loud.
4 He reads slowly. His reading is slow.

Double check! 1-6

1 1 She read the book, but she didn't enjoy it.
2 He went to the zoo and he saw an elephant.
3 They are tired because they stayed up late.
4 It is Saturday, so she isn't going to go to school.
5 They are friends, but they always argue!
2 1a goes b went c 's going
2a drop b 's dropping
3a 's buying b bought c buys
4a dyes b dyed c 's dying
3

Adjectives	Adverbs
bad	badly
brave	bravely
busy	busily
careful	carefully
dangerous	dangerously
easy	easily
gentle	gently
happy	happily
noisy	noisily
patient	patiently
slow	slowly
good	well

4 1 Speaking English is useful. Do you like speaking English?
2 Let's go camping. Camping in the countryside is fun.
3 He doesn't like visiting the dentist, but not visiting the dentist is bad for his teeth.
4 Eating junk food is expensive. Not eating junk food is healthy.
5 She likes cycling. Cycling fast is frightening.

Double check! 1–6

1 Make one sentence from two sentences. Use *and*, *but*, *or*, *so*.

1. She read the book. She didn't enjoy it.
   She read the book, but she didn't enjoy it.

2. He went to the zoo. He saw an elephant.
   _____
   _____

3. They are tired. They stayed up late.
   _____
   _____

4. It is Saturday. She isn't going to go to school.
   _____
   _____

5. They are friends. They always argue!
   _____
   _____

2 Complete the sentences with the present simple, present continuous or past simple.

1. **go**
   a. He *goes* _____ swimming every week.
   b. He _____ swimming last Friday.
   c. He _____ swimming today.

2. **drop**
   a. We never _____ litter.
   b. Look at him! He _____ litter.

3. **buy**
   a. She's hungry, so she _____ some food.
   b. She _____ some new clothes last week.
   c. She _____ sweets every day.

4. **dye**
   a. He often _____ his hair.
   b. Yesterday, he _____ his hair green!
   c. Now, he _____ his hair black.

3 Put the words below in the correct place and complete the chart.

bad brave busy carefully dangerously easy gentle
happy noisy patiently slowly well

Adjectives	Adverbs
bad	badly
_____	_____
_____	_____
_____	_____
_____	_____
_____	_____
_____	_____

4 Complete the sentences with the gerunds (affirmative or negative) of the verbs below.

camp cycle eat ~~speak~~ visit

1. *Speaking* _____ English is useful. Do you like _____ English?

2. Let's go _____ .
   _____ in the countryside is fun.

3. He doesn't like _____ the
   dentist, but _____ the
   dentist is bad for his teeth.

4. _____ junk food is
   expensive. _____ junk
   food is healthy.

5. She likes _____ .
   _____ fast is
   frightening.

7 Will you go to Mars?

Future *will*

Meaning
Will has several functions. Here *will* is used for stating future fact and making strong prediction. The boundary between these two common uses is often unclear as it frequently involves opinion.

Form
- The infinitive of the main verb, without *to*, is always used with *will*, except in short answers where the main verb is omitted.
- Questions are made by inverting *will* and subject.
- *Wh-* question words are placed before *will*.
- Contractions are generally used in spoken English (although full forms can be used for emphasis), and full forms are generally used in formal written English.
- *Will* is generally contracted to *'ll*. The negative contraction is won't, /wəʊnt/.

Vocabulary
Nouns: *air, astronaut, robot, spaceship, space station*
Verbs: *bring, save, send, will*
Adverbs: *inside, outside, perhaps*

Preview activity
Ask students *Are you interested in space travel? What do you know about space? What words do you know in English?* (For example, *planet, Earth, moon, star, sun*.)

▶ **Worksheet**

Student's Book answers
1b 1 no 2 yes 3 yes
2a + They**'ll** (**will**) **build** cities on the Moon.
   People **won't** (**will not**) **live** outside.
   ? **Will** you **go** to Mars?
   When will these things happen?
b + People **will travel** to Mars.
   – They **won't find** water on the Moon.
   ? **Will** we **live** in space?
   What **will** they **do**?
3 1 will live 2 will be 3 will fly 4 will visit 5 will do
   6 will have
4a 1 won't go 2 won't live 3 won't rain 4 won't be
   5 won't grow 6 won't die

Pairwork suggestion
Tell students to imagine that people will live in space. Tell them to predict other effects in their own life and life in general. In pairs, students write down five sentences with *will/won't*.

Student's Book answers
5 1 Where will we live?
   2 Why will we live inside?
   3 How will we travel?
   4 Who will build space stations?
   5 What will we find on Mars?
   6 When will it happen?

6 1 Will I visit other countries?
   2 No, you won't.
   3 What will I do?
   4 You will be an astronaut.
   5 You will travel/go to other planets.
   6 Will I go/travel to the Moon?
   7 No, you won't.
   8 You will go to Mars!
   9 Will I have a long life?
   10 Yes, you will.
   11 You will live to 100 –
   12 and you will have eleven children!
   13 No, I won't!

Pairwork suggestion
Students take it in turns to assume the role of the fortune teller. This is to practise speaking and asking questions – so the questioner leads the exchange.

Student's Book answers
7 Answers will vary.

Puzzle
On Bob's 21st birthday, Ali will be 17. He will be 21 in four more years' time; so if Celia is 19 in four years, she will be 23.

Writing extension
When your students have worked out the maths involved (drawing vertical lines with years marked on is helpful!), they can make similar puzzles of their own to give to a partner.

Worksheet

Use these activities before exercise 1 to preteach and to practise the vocabulary in the unit.

Answers
A 1 spaceship 2 space station 3 Earth 4 sun 5 stars
   6 astronaut 7 moon 8 planet 9 robot
B 1 outside 2 inside 3 to 4 by 5 in 6 on

Will you go to Mars?

Worksheet 7

A Write the names of the things in the picture.

astronaut   Earth   moon   planet   robot   ~~spaceship~~   space station   stars   sun

1 spaceship
2 _____
3 _____
4 _____
5 _____
6 _____
7 _____
8 _____
9 _____

B Complete these sentences about the picture with the prepositions below.

by   in   inside   on   ~~outside~~   to

1 The astronaut is _outside_ the spaceship.

2 The robot is _____ the spaceship.

3 They are flying _____ the space station.

4 They are travelling _____ spaceship.

5 The space station is _____ space.

6 Astronauts are building a second space station _____ the moon.

From **Grammar Works 2** by Mick Gammidge
© Cambridge University Press 1998

PHOTOCOPIABLE

19

8 We shouldn't waste energy

Should
To + infinitive for purpose

Should: Meaning
Should has several functions. Here *should* is used to express advice and obligation (but weaker than *must*); generally stating the sensible thing to do.

Form
The infinitive of the main verb is always used with *should*, except in short answers where the main verb is omitted.
- Questions are made by inverting *should* and subject.
- *Wh-* question words are placed before *should*.
- *Should* doesn't contract but is usually unstressed. The negative contraction – *shouldn't* – is generally used in spoken English (although the full form can be used for emphasis), and the full form is generally used in formal written English.

To + infinitive
This construction is used here to express reason for actions; it explains the purpose of the preceding verb. (*To* is not stressed, /tə/.)

Vocabulary
Nouns: *bath, coal, electricity, energy, gas, gate, goat, heat, light, pollution, shower, tap, wind*
Verbs: *cause, close, heat, recycle, should, turn off, waste*
Adjective: *glass*
Quantifiers: *all, most*

Preview activity
Preteach *pollution* (you might use photographs from newspaper articles) and ask students what they know about it. (Elicit, for example, *dirty, unhealthy*.)

▶ Worksheet

Student's Book answers
1b 1 bad 2 good 3 bad 4 good
2a People use wood to heat their homes.
People save energy to stop pollution.
Some people take showers to save hot water.
b Some countries **use** the wind **to make** energy.
3 1 use, to make
2 stayed up, to watch
3 's going to get up, to go
4 visits, to take
5 rides, to save
6 buy, to read
4a + We **should** take showers.
– We **shouldn't** travel by car.
? **Should** we save energy?
What **should** we do?
b + I should save energy.
– They shouldn't waste energy.
? Should we take baths?
How should we travel?
5 1 should close
2 should turn off
3 shouldn't drop
4 shouldn't drive
5 shouldn't play
6 shouldn't bite

Writing suggestion
Students read Unit 6, exercise 4 again and use the information to write advice for a healthy life style with *you should/shouldn't* (*to* + infinitive).

Student's Book answers
6 1 should think
2 should we do
3 to help
4 shouldn't waste
5 should turn off
6 should close
7 to keep
8 should use
9 should recycle
10 to save

7 Answers will vary.

Puzzle
First the man takes the goat to the other side of the river. Then he takes the dog BUT he takes the goat back with him to the start. Then he takes the apples across the river and leaves them with the dog. Finally, he takes the goat back across the river.

Groupwork suggestion
In small groups, students write letters to an advice column from a fictitious reader with a problem. Encourage students to use their imagination, as this is an opportunity to recycle the language they have learnt. Groups exchange letters and write replies giving advice with *should/shouldn't*.

Worksheet

Extra vocabulary: *basin*

Use these activities before exercise 1 to preteach and to practise the vocabulary in the unit.

Answers
A 1 wind 2 gas 3 coal 4 water 5 wood 6 electricity
7 food
B 1 light 2 fire 3 window 4 tap 5 basin 6 bath
7 shower

Extension activity
After exercise 6, ask students to look at the illustration for **B** again and say what is wrong, using *They should/shouldn't*.

We shouldn't waste energy

Worksheet 8

A Look at the pictures below and write the names of the forms of energy.

coal   electricity   food   gas   water   ~~wind~~   wood

1. wind
2. _____
3. _____
4. _____
5. _____
6. _____
7. _____

B Write the names of the things in the picture.

basin   bath   fire   ~~light~~   shower   tap   window

1. light
2. _____
3. _____
4. _____
5. _____
6. _____
7. _____

From **GRAMMAR WORKS 2** by Mick Gammidge
© Cambridge University Press 1998

9 Are you doing anything next Saturday?

Present continuous for future
Indefinite pronouns

Present continuous
Here the present continuous is used for future plans. It is often interchangeable with *going to*, the main difference being that we tend to use the present continuous rather than *going to* after a definite arrangement has been made.

Vocabulary
Verb: *arrive*
Adjective: *secret*
Indefinite pronouns: *anybody, anyone, anything, anywhere, everybody, everyone, everything, everywhere, no one, nobody, nothing, nowhere, somebody, someone, something, somewhere*

Student's Book answers
1 1 future   2 future

2 Indefinite pronouns

person	place	thing
somebody	somewhere	something
anybody	anywhere	anything
nobody	nowhere	nothing
everybody	everywhere	everything

(somebody = someone   anybody = anyone   nobody = no one   everybody = everyone)

3a + They're visiting **some**body.
   I'm going **some**where.
   – I'm not doing **any**thing.
   ? Are you doing **any**thing?

b + She's doing **something**.
   – We're not meeting **anybody**.
   He's not going **anywhere**.
   ? Is he going **anywhere**?
   Are you meeting **anybody**?

4 1 someone   2 anywhere   3 something   4 everywhere
   5 Everything   6 Nothing   7 Nowhere

5 1 she's arriving
   2 she's practising
   3 she's watching
   4 are meeting
   5 she's playing
   6 are flying

Classwork suggestion
Students draw an empty double-page diary as in the unit. They think of three things they want to do in the evenings and write them in their diary. Students move around and make arrangements to do their own activities and other students' activities together until their diary is full. The target language is present continuous for future and indefinite pronouns, e.g. *Are you doing anything on Monday? Yes, I am. I'm doing something / meeting someone, going somewhere. / No, I'm not. What are you doing?* It would be a good idea to first quickly revise useful language like *Let's ... , How about ...?* etc.

Student's Book answers
6 1 Are you doing anything next week?
   2 Yes, I'm going to London.
   3 Are you playing tennis with anyone?
   4 I'm playing on Friday with someone.
   5 Are you going anywhere after London?
   6 No, I'm coming home to the USA.

Groupwork extension
Using the conversation in exercise 6 as a model, in small groups, students roleplay an interview between a sports star and sports reporters. Students choose which sports star they want to be.

Student's Book answers
7 Answers will vary.

Puzzle
The question has to ask one computer what the other computer would say: 'Does the other computer say that it/you lie/s? / tell/s the truth?' The answer is always the opposite of the truth.

▶ *Worksheet*

Worksheet

Use these activities at the end of the unit to review days of the week, months of the year and seasons.

Answers

A 1 Sunday   2 Monday   3 Tuesday   4 Wednesday
   5 Thursday   6 Friday   7 Saturday

B 1 January   2 February   3 March   4 April   5 May   6 June
   7 July   8 August   9 September   10 October   11 November
   12 December

C 1 spring   2 summer   3 autumn   4 winter

Extension activity
Use the worksheet as an opportunity to review appropriate use of prepositions, e.g. *on Monday, in March, in spring*. Students make sentences, using indefinite pronouns if possible, e.g. *On Sunday nobody goes to school*.

Are you doing anything next Saturday?

Worksheet 9

A Most days of the week in English come from the old Norse language. Write the English names for the days.

1. The sun's day. **Sunday**
2. The moon's day. _____
3. Tyr's day. (Tyr was the Norse god of the planet Mars.) _____
4. Wodin's day. (Wodin was king of the Norse gods.) _____
5. Thor's day. (Thor was the Norse god of thunder.) _____
6. Frig's day. (Frig was Wodin's wife.) _____
7. The planet Saturn's day. _____

B Write the names of the months on the calendar below.

1 _____	2 _____	3 _____	4 _____	5 ___	6 ____
1 2 3 4 5 6 7 8 9 10 11 12 13 14 15 16 17 18 19 20 21 22 23 24 25 (26) 27 28 29 30 31	1 2 3 4 5 6 7 8 9 10 11 (12) 13 14 15 16 17 18 19 20 21 22 23 24 25 26 27 28	1 2 3 4 5 6 7 8 9 10 11 12 13 14 15 16 17 18 19 20 21 22 23 24 25 26 27 28 29 30 31	1 2 3 4 5 6 7 8 9 10 11 12 13 14 15 16 17 18 19 20 21 22 23 24 25 26 27 28 29 30	1 2 3 4 5 6 7 8 9 10 11 12 13 14 15 16 17 18 19 20 21 22 23 24 25 26 27 28 29 30 31	1 2 3 4 5 6 7 8 9 (10) 11 12 13 14 15 16 17 18 19 20 21 22 (23) 24 25 26 27 28 29 30
7 ____	**8 _____**	**9 _____**	**10 _____**	**11 _____**	**12 _____**
1 2 3 4 5 6 7 8 9 10 11 12 13 14 15 16 17 18 19 20 21 22 23 24 25 26 27 28 29 30 31	1 2 3 4 (5) 6 (7) 8 9 10 11 12 13 14 15 16 17 18 19 20 21 22 23 24 25 26 27 28 29 30 31	1 2 3 4 5 6 7 8 9 10 11 12 13 14 15 16 17 18 19 20 21 22 23 24 25 26 27 28 29 30	1 2 3 4 5 6 7 8 9 10 11 12 (13) 14 15 16 17 18 19 20 21 22 23 24 25 26 27 28 29 30 31	1 2 3 4 5 6 7 8 9 10 11 12 13 14 15 16 17 18 19 20 21 22 23 24 25 26 27 28 29 30	1 2 3 4 5 6 7 8 9 10 11 12 13 14 15 16 17 18 19 20 21 22 23 24 25 26 27 28 29 30 31

C Look at the pictures of England. Write the seasons (times of year).

1 ___spring___   2 _____   3 _____   4 _____

10 There aren't enough girls

Countable and uncountable nouns
Too (much/many), Enough / Not enough

Countable and uncountable nouns
This is an opportunity to revise countable and uncountable nouns from *Grammar Works 1* Unit 9.

Too (much/many), enough / not enough
Draw students' attention to the differences in word order between the constructions using *(not) enough* + noun and those using *(not)* + adjective + *enough*.

Vocabulary
enough, not enough, too much
Nouns: *bucket, cheese, jumper, omelette, onion, pepper, salad, salt, tomato*
Verb: *turn up*

Student's Book answers
1b 1 yes 2 yes 3 no
 c enough – b
   too much – c
   not enough – a
2a 1 There**'s enough** salad.
   2 There **aren't enough** girls.
   3 There**'s too much** sugar in it.
   4 There **are too many** boys.
 b 1 There **are** too **many** sandwiches.
   2 There **are** not **enough** boys.
   3 There **are** too **many** girls.
   4 There **is** not **enough** sugar.
3a   Countable   Uncountable
   cheese   ✓
   eggs   ✓
   milk   ✓
   onions   ✓
   salt/pepper   ✓
   tomatoes   ✓
 b 1 There are too many eggs.
   2 There are enough tomatoes.
   3 There's not / There isn't enough cheese.
   4 There are too many onions.
   5 There's too much milk.

▶ Worksheet
Student's Book answers
4a 1 It's too sweet.
   2 It's not loud enough.
 b 1c 2a 3b
   1 It isn't hot enough.
   2 It's too hot.
   3 It's hot enough.
5 1 It's sweet enough.
   2 It's too difficult.
   3 He's not old enough.
   4 It's big enough.
   5 The rabbit is too fast.
   6 She's not tidy enough.
   7 He's not tall enough.

6 1 There's too much sugar. It's too sweet.
   2 There isn't / There's not enough cold water in the bath. It's too hot.
   3 There aren't enough pictures in the book. It's too serious.
   4 There are too many rainy days in Britain. It's not sunny enough.
   5 There's too much water in the buckets. They're too heavy.
7 Answers will vary.

Classwork extension
Ask students about the town where they live (or are studying in now, if that is different). Collate students' opinions by asking questions like *Who thinks that there are not enough / enough / too many cinemas / shops / parks / cars / buses / interesting places, etc. in town?* Ask for a show of hands and write the numbers for each answer on the board. Students then write generalised statements about the class, either individually or in pairs, e.g. *Most students think that there are not enough cinemas in town*.

Student's Book answers
Puzzle

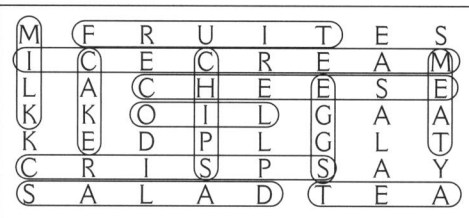

Extension activities
If your students enjoy this kind of word puzzle, they can write their own word grids and exchange them with their partner.

> ### Worksheet
> Use this activity after exercise 3 to revise food vocabulary.
>
> **Answers**
> 1 apple 2 bacon 3 banana 4 beans 5 biscuit 6 burger
> 7 cake 8 cheese 9 chicken 10 chips 11 coconut
> 12 coffee 13 crisps 14 egg 15 fish 16 fruit 17 ice cream 18 lemon 19 meat 20 omelette 21 onion
> 22 orange 23 pasta 24 pepper 25 pizza 26 salad
> 27 salt 28 sandwich 29 sausage 30 sugar 31 tomato
> 32 vegetables
>
> **Extension activity**
> Students decide if each item in the food word list is countable or uncountable.

There aren't enough girls

Worksheet 10

Make a food picture dictionary. Write the names of the things below.
(You can look at the words at the bottom of the page for help.)

 1 apple	 2 _____	 3 _____	 4 _____
 5 _____	 6 _____	 7 _____	 8 _____
 9 _____	 10 _____	 11 _____	 12 _____
 13 _____	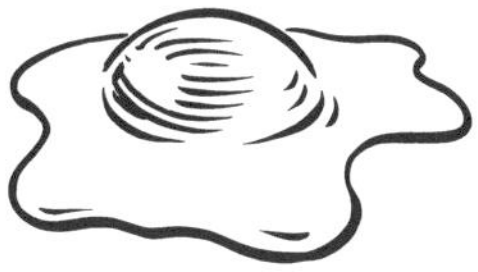 14 _____	 15 _____	 16 _____
 17 _____	 18 _____	 19 _____	 20 _____
 21 _____	 22 _____	 23 _____	 24 _____
 25 _____	 26 _____	 27 _____	 28 _____
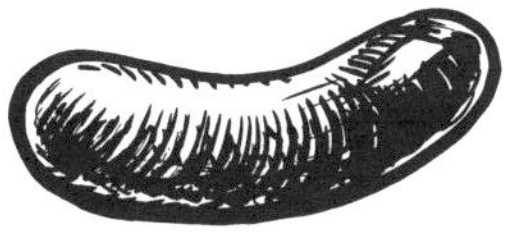 29 _____	 30 _____	 31 _____	 32 _____

fruit cheese orange sugar coffee ~~apple~~ biscuit ice cream bacon chicken egg burger
vegetables pepper salad lemon cake sausage tomato fish banana pasta onion salt meat
pizza sandwich chips crisps beans omelette coconut

From **GRAMMAR WORKS 2** by Mick Gammidge
© Cambridge University Press 1998

PHOTOCOPIABLE

11 The biggest in the world!

Comparative and superlative adjectives, as ... as, not as ... as, ... than, the ...

Meaning
Although the construction *not* + comparative + *than* exists in English, it is best avoided at this level as it is ambiguous. *X is not bigger than Y* can mean that *X is smaller than Y* or *as big as Y*.

Form
Comparatives and superlative adjectives with more than one syllable are usually formed with *more* and *most*, rather than *-er* and *-est*, except for words ending in *-y*. (Certain two syllable words can take either form, e.g. *clever*.) The definite article is used with the superlative because the noun is unique.

Spelling
Spelling rules for regular comparative and superlative forms are:
– When the adjective ends in two or more consonants, or ends in two or more vowels and then one consonant, add *-er/-est*, e.g. *longer, cleanest*.
– When the adjective ends in one vowel and one consonant, double the consonant and add *-er/-est*, e.g. *bigger*.
– But adjectives ending in *-w, -y* or *-x* do *not* double, e.g. *newer*.
– When the adjective ends in *-e*, add *-r/-st*, e.g. *largest*.
– When the adjective has two syllables and ends in *-y*, change *-y* to *-i* and add *-er/-est*, e.g. *heavier*.

Pronunciation
The ending, *-er*, is pronounced /ə/: *r* is not pronounced in standard British English unless it is followed by a vowel sound.
• The *-est* ending is pronounced /ɪst/ or /əst/ but not /est/.
• In constructions with *(not) as* + adjective + *as*, *as* is pronounced /əz/.

Vocabulary
Nouns: *dinosaur, giraffe*
Adjectives: *large, nice*
The names of the following dinosaurs are not key words, but the approximate pronunciations are: /ʌltrəsɔːrəs/, /brækiəʊsɔːrəs/, /mæmenkisɔːrəs/, /taɪrænəsɔːrəs/, /kɒmpsəgneɪʃəs/.

Preview activity
Ask students what they know about dinosaurs in their own language. Ask them if they know any English vocabulary, e.g. any appropriate adjectives, they could use to talk about dinosaurs.

Student's Book answers
1 1 b 2 c 3 a
2a

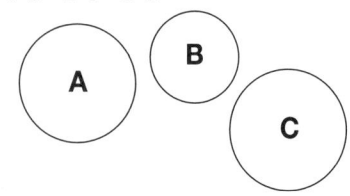

b 1 B is smaller than C. 2 A isn't as small as B.
c big + -ger/-gest   large + -r/-st   long + -er/-est
heavy + -ier/-iest   tall + -er/-est

3
cheap	cheaper	the cheapest
fast	faster	the fastest
friendly	friendlier	the friendliest
hot	hotter	the hottest
nice	nicer	the nicest
small	smaller	the smallest

Worksheet A and B
Groupwork suggestion
Put students into groups of about five. Tell them to arrange themselves into a line by age. (They ask: *How old are you? When is your birthday?*) One student from each group reports to the class, stating the oldest and the youngest and making comparisons. (You can repeat this activity using other adjectives if they are not too sensitive for your students.)

Student's Book answers
4 1 A whale is bigger than a monkey.
2 An elephant is not as tall as a giraffe.
3 A tortoise is slower than a cat.
4 A cat is not as fast as a cheetah.
5 A dog is friendlier than a lion.
6 A mouse is smaller than a tortoise.
7 A monkey is not as strong as an elephant.

Worksheet C and D
Pairwork suggestion
In pairs, students write similar sentences using different nouns.

Student's Book answers
5 were (1), larger (2), than (3), taller (4), than (5), was (6), the (7), smallest (8), was (9), as (10), as (11), was (12), the (13), biggest (14), wasn't (15), as (16), as (17), is (18), the (19), largest (20),
6 1 London is the biggest city.
2 The Severn is the longest river.
3 Canary Wharf is the tallest building.
4 Oxford is the oldest university.
5 Elizabeth II is the richest person.
7 Answers will vary.

Project work suggestion
Groups choose another country and research it to make a poster involving features like those in exercise 7, e.g. *highest mountain*, etc. The class can make a picture poster of their findings.

Student's Book answers
Puzzle
Australia! (It was the biggest regardless of when it was found by Cook.)

Worksheet

Extra vocabulary: *light* (adj)

A and B Students can do these activities after exercise 3.

Answers
1a colder; cold; coldest b hot, hotter, hottest 2a light, lighter, lightest b heavy, heavier, heaviest 3a smallest, small, smaller b large, largest, larger 4a long, longer, longest b shortest, short, shorter 5a taller, tallest, tall b short, shorter, shortest 6a younger, youngest, young b older, oldest, old

C and D Students can do these activities after exercise 4.

Answers
C 1 cat 2 cheetah 3 dog 4 elephant 5 giraffe 6 lion 7 monkey 8 mouse 9 tortoise
D brave 6 clever 7 fast 2 friendly 3 lazy 1 slow 9 small 8 strong 4 tall 5

The biggest in the world! Worksheet 11

A Match these words with the pictures. Write the comparative and superlative forms.

~~cold~~ hot light heavy small large long short tall young

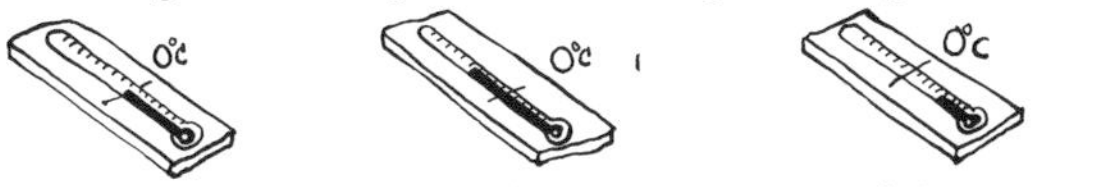

1a colder   cold   coldest
1b _____ _____ _____ 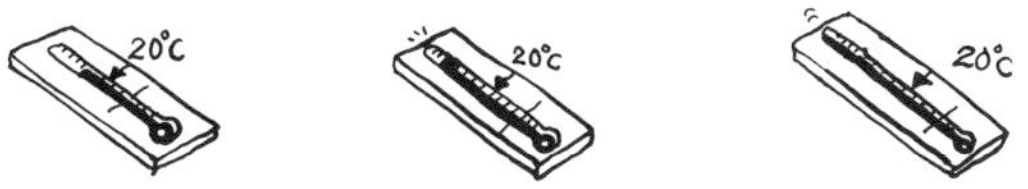
2a _____ _____ _____ 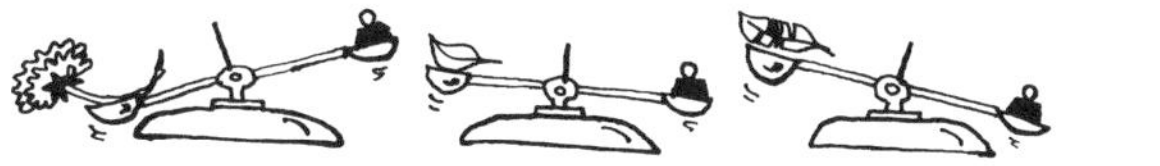
2b _____ _____ _____ 
3a _____ _____ _____ 
3b _____ _____ _____ 
4a _____ _____ _____ 
4b _____ _____ _____ 
5a _____ _____ _____ 
5b _____ _____ _____
6a _____ _____ _____ 
6b _____ _____ _____

B Write the opposites of 5a and 6a for 5b and 6b. Draw pictures.

C Label the pictures below. (You can use a dictionary.)

1 cat 
2 _____ 
3 _____ 
4 _____ 
5 _____ 
6 _____ 
7 _____ 
8 _____ 
9 _____

D Now match these adjectives with the animals in activity C.

brave _____   clever _____   fast _____   friendly _____   lazy 1

slow _____   small _____   strong _____   tall _____

From GRAMMAR WORKS 2 by Mick Gammidge
© Cambridge University Press 1998

PHOTOCOPIABLE

12 It's the best!

Comparative and superlative adjectives with *more* and *most*

- Students' ability to recognise and count syllables is important here. It may be useful to clap or tap out the syllables and encourage students to do the same. (It is also an opportunity to focus on word stress.)
- We use *more* and *most* with adjectives with two or more syllables (but not adjectives ending in -y).
- Some adjectives are irregular, for example:

good	better	the best
bad	worse	the worst
far	further	the furthest

Pronunciation
More is usually pronounced /mɔː/. The -r in *more* is not usually pronounced in standard British English unless it is followed by a vowel sound.

Vocabulary
Nouns: *castle, ghost, hotel*
Adjectives: *best, better, cheap, further, furthest, intelligent, peaceful, polite, romantic, worse, worst*

Preview activity
Ask students *What do you do in your holidays? Do you go to different places?* Students look at the tourist brochure in exercise 1a. Ask *Do you like the places in the pictures?* Use the pictures to preteach *castle, hotel, peaceful, romantic.*

Student's Book answers
1b Black Swan ** – ****
  Sunlaws House *****
2 beautiful 3 exciting 3
  expensive 3 far 1
  friendly 2 interesting 3 (4)
  peaceful 2 quiet 2
  romantic 3 small 1
 b beautiful, exciting, expensive, interesting, peaceful, romantic

3
adjective	comparative	superlative
boring	more boring	most boring
exciting	more exciting	most exciting
far	further	furthest
friendly	friendlier	friendliest
good	better	best
intelligent	more intelligent	most intelligent
polite	more polite	most polite
quiet	quieter	quietest
serious	more serious	most serious
bad	worse	worst

4 1 cheaper than 2 not as cheap as 3 the most peaceful
  4 the furthest 5 more interesting 6 the best

Groupwork activity
Bring holiday brochures to class and give one to each group. Ask students to decide where they want to go as a group and give at least five reasons for their choice, using comparative and superlative sentences. Alternatively, tell groups to discuss where they want to go for a trip in your town/country and come to an agreement. Again, they give at least five reasons for their choice, using comparative and superlative sentences.

Student's Book answers
5 1 The Ford is older than the Porsche.
 2 The Porsche is more exciting than the Ford.
 3 The Ford is not as comfortable as the Porsche.
 4 The Porsche is faster than the Ford.
 5 The Porsche is not as long as the Ford.
6 Answers will vary.
7 Answers will vary.

Pairwork activity
In pairs, students compare their ideas. They then agree on one or two new adjectives to compare each pair of nouns in the exercise and write sentences.

Student's Book answers
Puzzle
The lines are all the same length.

▶ Worksheet

Worksheet

Use these activities at the end of the unit to review adjectives and building/place names.

Answers
A 1 peaceful 2 quiet 3 romantic 4 comfortable 5 expensive
  6 cheap 7 dangerous 8 exciting 9 interesting

Extension activity
Students write sentences about the holidays using the adjectives in comparative and superlative forms. They compare their ideas with a partner.

Answers
B 1 bank 2 car park 3 castle 4 flat 5 hotel 6 house
  7 museum 8 newsagent 9 post office 10 restaurant
  11 school 12 shop 13 supermarket 14 university 15 zoo

It's the best!

Worksheet 12

A Look at the pictures of four holidays. Put the adjectives below with the pictures.

cheap   comfortable   dangerous   exciting   expensive   interesting   ~~peaceful~~   quiet   romantic

1 peaceful   4 _____   6 _____   7 _____

2 _____   5 _____   8 _____

3 _____   9 _____

B Make a buildings and places picture dictionary. Write the names of the things in the pictures below. (You can look at the words at the bottom of the page for help.)

1 bank   2 _____   3 _____

4 _____   5 _____   6 _____

7 _____   8 _____   9 _____

10 _____   11 _____   12 _____

13 _____   14 _____   15 _____

restaurant ~~bank~~ shop newsagent zoo castle flat post office school hotel supermarket car park museum university house

From GRAMMAR WORKS 2 by Mick Gammidge
© Cambridge University Press 1998

PHOTOCOPIABLE

29

Check point 7–12

1 1 will see 2 won't turn on 3 will find 4 will tell 5 won't be 6 will shout

2
1 He should pick up the litter to tidy the room.
2 He should take the glasses to the kitchen to wash them.
3 He should telephone the video shop to ask about the video.
4 He should go to the shop to buy a new bowl.
5 He should visit the neighbours to give them a present.

3
– Are you doing (1) anything (2) this afternoon? My parents are coming (3) home this evening and everywhere (4) is untidy.
– I'm doing (5) something (6) at 2.
– What are you doing (7)?
– I'm having (8) a piano lesson.
– Liam, please help. The house is untidy! Sue is going (9) somewhere (10). I telephoned Kim's house but no one (11) was at home. My parents are arriving (12) at about 6.
– I'm not doing (13) anything (14). I'll see you in 20 minutes.

4
1 There are too many clouds. It's not / It isn't sunny enough.
2 There isn't enough milk in this coffee. It's too strong.
3 There is too much oil in my food. It's not / It isn't healthy enough.
4 There are too many questions in my homework. It's too difficult.
5 There aren't enough people to move the piano. It's too heavy.

5
1 was not as strong as
2 was more frightening
3 was not as dangerous as
4 was smaller than
5 was not as heavy as
6 was noisier than

6
1 is the longest
2 is longer than
3 isn't as long as
4 is higher than
5 isn't as high as
6 is the highest

Double check! 1–6

1
1 He should use suncream.
2 He shouldn't use oil.
3 He should wear sunglasses and a hat.
4 He should drink some water.
5 He shouldn't sit in the sun at noon.
6 He should go inside!

2
1 anybody
2 Everybody/Everyone
3 anywhere
4 something
5 anyone/anybody
6 No one/Nobody
7 nothing

3
1 There will be too much pollution.
2 There will be too many cars.
3 There will be too many people.
4 There won't be enough food.
5 There won't be enough water.
6 There won't be enough clean air.

4
1 A is worse than B.
2 A is not as bad as C.
3 C is the worst.
4 A is the most beautiful.
5 B is not as beautiful as A.
6 B is more beautiful than C.
7 A is not as big as B.
8 B is the biggest.
9 B is bigger than C.

Double check! 7–12

1 Look at the boy in the picture. What is he doing wrong? Write sentences with *should/shouldn't* and the verbs below.

drink go sit ~~use~~ use wear

1 ____*He should use*____ suncream.
2 _____ oil.
3 _____ sunglasses and a hat.
4 _____ some water.
5 _____ in the sun at noon.
6 _____ inside!

2 Complete the sentences below with indefinite pronouns.

1 It's a secret. Don't tell ____*anybody*____!
2 _____ knows that smoking is bad for you.
3 Are you going _____ at the weekend?
4 I met her at the shops. She was buying _____ for her mum's birthday.
5 Does _____ know the answer?
6 _____ is as tall as Paulo. He's the tallest.
7 He's very lazy. He does _____ every day.

3 Look at a scientist's ideas about the year 2,500. Complete the sentences with *there will/won't* and *not enough / too much/many*.

1 ____*There will be too much*____ pollution.

2 _____ cars.

3 _____ people.

4 _____ food.

5 _____ water.

6 _____ clean air.

4 Complete the sentences about the pictures. Use comparatives and superlatives of the adjectives.

bad
1 A ____*is worse than*____ B.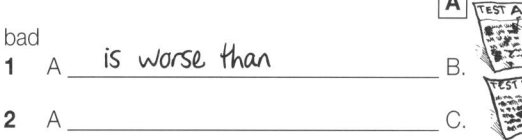
2 A _____ C.
3 C _____ .

beautiful
4 A _____ .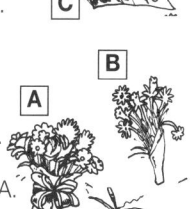
5 B _____ A.
6 B _____ C.

big
7 A _____ B.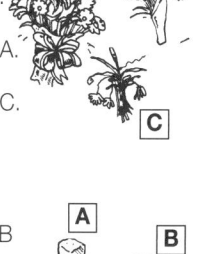
8 B _____ .
9 B _____ C.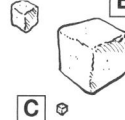

13 It was rising from the sea

Past continuous past simple contrast with *while/when*

Meaning
Here the past continuous is used to describe an action in progress around a point in time in the past, or an action in progress which was interrupted by another event.

Form
- For interrupted actions, either *while* is used at the beginning of the continuous clause and a comma is placed at the end, or *when* is used at the beginning of the simple clause.
- The past continuous is formed with the past simple of *be* as an auxiliary verb and the present participle of the main verb.
- The negatives are usually contracted in spoken English, *wasn't/weren't*, but full forms are used in written English.

Pronunciation
The auxiliary *was/were* is generally an unstressed weak form: /wəz/ or /wə/ though the strong form can be used for emphasis: /wɒz/ or /wɜː/. Negatives do not have a weak form: /wɒznt/, /wɜːnt/.

Vocabulary
Nouns: *distance, fisherman, monster, sack*
Verb: *rise*
Conjunctions: *when, while*
Preposition: *near*

Student's Book answers
1b 1 past 2 no 3 an island
2a + They **were** look**ing** at a new island.
  – They **weren't** look**ing** at a boat.
  While they were fishing**,** they saw something.
  They were sailing nearer **when** it suddenly grew larger.
  b + They **were** sail**ing** in the Atlantic.
  – The island **wasn't** grow**ing** smaller.
  They were fishing **when** they saw something.
  While they were sailing nearer**,** it grew larger.
3 1 were fishing
  2 was eating
  3 were drinking
  4 was standing up.
  5 were sitting down.
  6 was rising
4 Ann, Bill and Colin <u>were walking</u> in Scotland last Saturday, when something strange happened. At about 2 o'clock, <u>Ann was taking photos. Bill and Colin were collecting stones</u> when suddenly a monster appeared. It <u>was running from the forest</u> and <u>looking at them angrily</u>.
  1 They weren't walking. They were fishing.
  2 Ann wasn't taking photos. She was eating a sandwich.
  3 Bill and Colin weren't collecting stones. They were drinking tea.
  4 It wasn't running from the forest. It was rising from the water.
  5 It wasn't looking at them angrily. It was smiling / looking at their food.

▶ *Worksheet*

Pairwork suggestion
In pairs, students write their own sentences with the past continuous and *when/while* with the two clauses on separate pieces of paper. Collect the papers with the second clauses on them and redistribute them among the students. Students read their pieces of paper to each other and match up their sentences.

Student's Book answers
5 1 Kim was playing with her sister's baby when it bit her.
  2 While Sue was playing with her rabbit, it bit her.
  3 While the friends were fishing, it started to rain.
  4 The friends were fishing when it started to rain.
  5 While James was cycling home, his bike broke.
6 1 She was walking to school when she met a friend.
  2 The dog was eating his lunch when he came into the room.
  3 While they were writing on the board, the teacher arrived.
  4 While she was singing, the window broke.

Groupwork suggestion
Bring photos/pictures of busy scenes to class and tell students that the photo was taken at a point in the past, e.g. at 7.00 pm yesterday. (You could use the picture in Check point 1–6 exercise 2, reminding students that this happened at the time students did the Check point unit and so it is now in the past.) Students write sentences about what the people in the photo (or picture) were doing.

Student's Book answers
7 Answers will vary.

Puzzle
Only the speaker – all the others were coming from St Ives!

> ### Worksheet
>
> Use these activities after exercise 4 (before Pairwork suggestion) to review verbs. Activity A reviews verbs students know with *up* (to introduce and focus on two-part/phrasal verbs). Activity B reviews potentially mutually-confusing verbs.
>
> #### Answers
> **A** 1 get up 2 stand up 3 stay up 4 turn up 5 wake up
>
> **B** 1a see b look for c look at d watch
>   2a arrive b go c come
>   3a carry b bring c take

It was rising from the sea — Worksheet 13

A Look at the pictures. Write five verbs with *up*.

1 _____
2 _____
3 _____
4 _____
5 _____

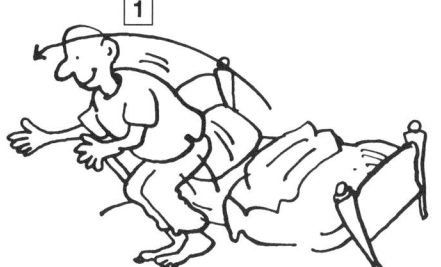
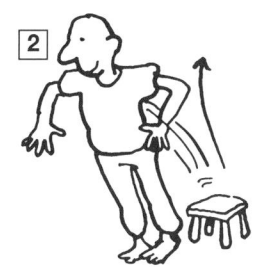

B Match the verbs below with the pictures.

1 look at   look for   ~~see~~   watch

a ___see___   b _____   c _____   d _____

2 arrive   come   go

a _____   b _____   c _____

3 bring   carry   take

a _____   b _____   c _____

From **GRAMMAR WORKS 2** by Mick Gammidge
© Cambridge University Press 1998

14 Which one was driving?

Past continuous question forms
Which ... ?
One/Ones

Past continuous
Questions in the past continuous are formed by putting the auxiliary *be* before the subject. *Wh-* question words are placed before the auxiliary.

Which ... ?
Which is usually used in questions about people and things when the choice of possible answers is restricted, or when all the possible choices are known. It is often used with pronouns *one/ones*, e.g. *Which one do you want?*

Vocabulary
Nouns: *accident, bicycle, bus driver, footprint, phone, police officer, seat belt, traffic lights*
Verbs: *cross, hit, remember*
Adjectives: *orange, red, yellow*

▶ **Worksheet A**

Preview activity
Ask students to look at the picture and name all the things they can in English. Elicit/Preteach *accident*.

Student's Book answers
1b 1 false
    2 true
2a 1 **Where were** you stand**ing**?   Next to the telephones.
    2 **Who was** driv**ing**?   The short man.
    3 **Was** he driv**ing** fast?   Yes, he was.
 b 1 **Who** was stand**ing** next to the telephones?   Sue.
    2 **Were** the men speak**ing** quietly to the bus driver?   No, they weren't.
    3 **What were** they argu**ing** about?   The accident.
3 1 Was he driving fast?   Yes, he was.
    2 Were they waiting at the lights?   No, they weren't.
    3 Was he watching the road?   No, he wasn't.
    4 Was he reading a newspaper?   Yes, he was.
    5 Was he talking to his friends?   Yes, he was.
    6 Was he wearing a seat belt?   No, he wasn't.
4a 1 one 2 ones 3 ones 4 one
 b 1 Which, one
    2 Which, ones
5 1 Which boy was carrying the orange juice?   The one in the green shirt.
    2 Which girl was throwing balls at coconuts?   The one in the yellow shirt.
    3 Which girls were climbing the wall?   The ones in the orange shirts.
    4 Which boys were jumping?   The ones in the red shirts.
6 1 Who was sleeping?
    2 Where was the old man lying?
    3 What was the dog doing?
    4 Who was carrying the orange juice?

▶ **Worksheet B**

Class activity
Preteach the noun *power cut*. Give students a context, e.g. tell them they are all office workers, and ask them to mime one activity they would do in an office. Tell them that when you clap your hands, they are to imagine that the electricity has been cut so everything stops. They then ask another student the question *What were you doing when the power cut happened?* and reply to the questions with the past continuous. Repeat the activity (with different contexts perhaps, such as in the home) for as long as you think it is interesting for your students.

Student's Book answers
7 Answers will vary.

Pairwork suggestion
Students practise asking and answering the questions in activity 7 in pairs and then ask similar questions substituting different times.

Student's Book answers

Puzzle

Worksheet

A Use this activity before the preview activity to preteach *traffic lights, phones, bus driver*.

Answers
1 traffic lights 2 bus driver 3 bus 4 phones 5 car park
6 bus stop 7 map 8 park 9 post box 10 police officer

B Use this activity after exercise 6 for consolidation of names of colours.

Answers
Check these with the class by holding up coloured items (crayons, pieces of paper, etc.) and elicit words and spellings from the class. Write each word on the board so that students can mark their own answers.

Extension activity
Ask students: *Which colours make green/purple/orange/grey/brown?* Elicit responses: *Yellow and blue make green. Blue and red make purple. Red and yellow make orange. Black and white make grey. Red, blue and yellow make brown.*

Students practise asking and answering the questions in pairs.

Which one was driving?

Worksheet 14

A Write the names of the things in the picture.

1. traffic lights
2. _____
3. _____
4. _____
5. _____
6. _____
7. _____
8. _____
9. _____
10. _____

B Colour the diagram.

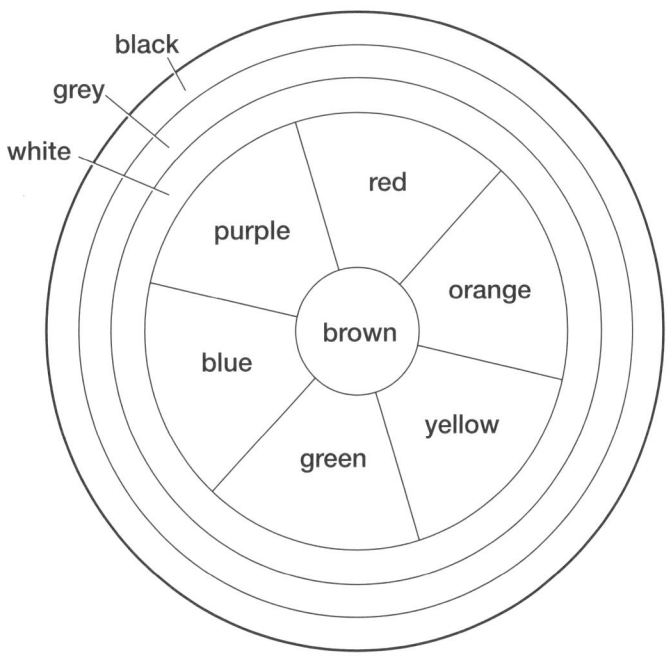

15 He is the pilot that built the smallest plane

Relative pronouns *who, which, that* in defining relative clauses

Form
Who is used for people in both subject and object position (*whom* is very rarely used in modern English except in extremely formal contexts); *which* is used for things, and *that* can be used for either.

Pronunciation
Pronouns are generally unstressed in English and *that* is a weak form: /ðət/.

Vocabulary
Nouns: balloon, helicopter, parrot, pilot, plane, submarine, vehicle, wheel, wing

▶ *Worksheet*

Student's Book answers
1b 1 T 2 F 3 T
2a 1 He is the pilot that built the smallest plane.
 2 *Concorde* is a passenger plane that can fly at 2,300 kilometres an hour.
b 1 *Bumble Bee* is a plane that is only 2.6 metres long.
 2 The Wright brothers were the pilots that flew the first plane.
3 1 Amy Johnson was a pilot that flew from England to Australia in 1930.
 2 The Montgolfier brothers were inventors that made the first passenger balloon.
 3 *Viking* is a space ship that went to Mars.
 4 A helicopter is a plane that hasn't got wings!

Pairwork suggestion
In pairs, students write similar sets of sentences (you could give them a different topic, e.g. animals) and swap their sentences with another pair to join with *that*.

Student's Book answers
4a 1 who 2 which
 b 1 who 2 which
 c that   person   who
    that   thing   which
5 1 A cyclist is a person who rides a bike.
 2 A cycle is a vehicle which has got two wheels.
 3 A pilot is a person who flies planes.
 4 A plane is a vehicle which travels in the air.
 5 A bus driver is a person who drives a bus.
 6 A bus is a vehicle which carries passengers.
6 1 A spaceship is something which / that travels in space.
 2 A doctor is someone who / that helps sick people.
 3 A sailor is someone who / that sails ships.
 4 A camera is something which / that takes photographs.
 5 A submarine is something which / that sails under the sea.

Pairwork suggestion
In pairs, students think of other definitions as in the exercise. You could give a broad area, e.g. jobs. Students jumble the nouns and definitions and swap them with another pair to match and then write sentences with *who* and *which*.

Extension activity
For speaking practice, students can chain questions and answers (either around the class or in groups) asking for definitions and answering, for example:
A: *What's a secretary?*
B: *A secretary is a person who types letters. What's a ship?*
C: *A ship is a thing which sails on the sea. What's a … ?*

Student's Book answers
7 Answers will vary.

Puzzle
The parrot can't hear – it's deaf.

Worksheet
Use this activity before exercise 1 to elicit / preteach *balloon, helicopter, passenger, pilot, plane, submarine, wheel, wing* and revise other forms of transport.

Answers
1 aeroplane a wing b passenger c pilot d wheel
2 balloon 3 bicycle 4 boat 5 bus 6 car 7 helicopter
8 motorbike 9 ship 10 submarine 11 train

He is the pilot that built the smallest plane

15

Make a transport picture dictionary. Write the names of the things below.
(You can look at the words at the bottom of the page for help.)

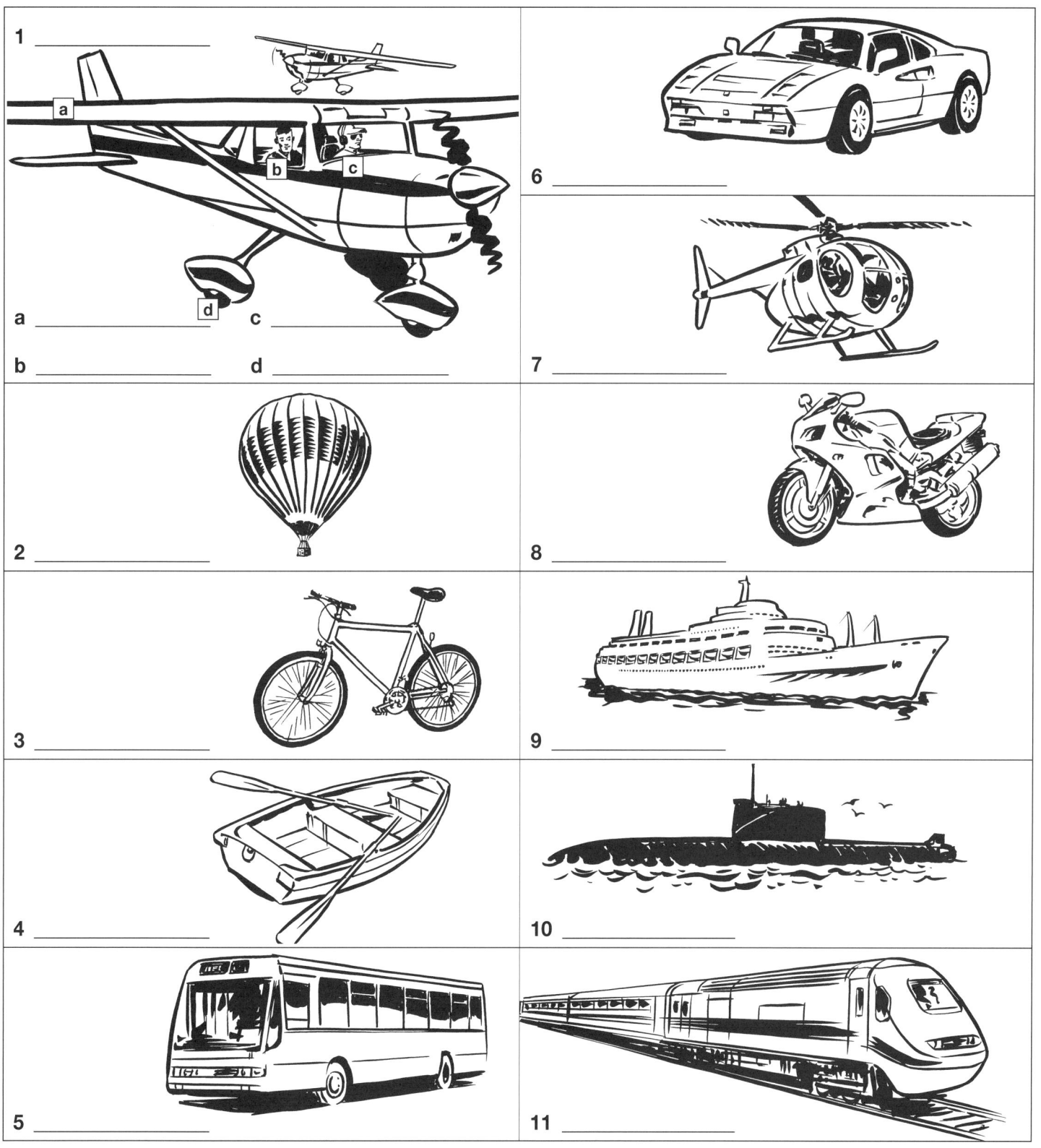

aeroplane wing bicycle
train balloon helicopter wheel boat pilot submarine passenger motorbike car ship bus

From **GRAMMAR WORKS 2** by Mick Gammidge
© Cambridge University Press 1998

PHOTOCOPIABLE

37

16 I really enjoyed myself

Reflexive and emphatic pronouns
Each other

Reflexive and emphatic pronouns
- Reflexive pronouns are object pronouns used when the object and subject are the same. Verbs used reflexively vary from language to language. In English *wash* and *dress* are not generally reflexive; we usually use *get*, e.g. *I got washed*.
- Emphatic pronouns are used to emphasise the subject and are placed after the object or objects (which are different from the subject).

Each other
Students sometimes confuse *themselves* with *each other*, missing the reciprocal meaning of *each other*, e.g. *They met themselves.

Pronunciation
The stress falls on *-self* in these pronouns and on *other* in *each other*.

Vocabulary
Reflexive/emphatic pronouns: *herself, himself, itself, myself, ourselves, themselves, yourself, yourselves*
Verbs: *feed, pay, point, repair*
Nouns: *(football) match, mirror, tape*
Object pronoun: *each other*

▶ **Worksheet**
Preview activity
You can introduce students to some of the emphatic pronouns by asking *Who does your/his/her homework? Does your mother/father do your homework?* (These questions should elicit answers that state that the students do it.) You can then make follow up comments like, *So, you do it yourself/he does it himself/she does it herself*.

1 1 T 2 F
2
object pronouns	reflexive pronouns
me	myself
you (👤)	yourself
him	himself
her	herself
it	itself
we	ourselves
you (👥+)	yourselves
them	themselves

3 1 b 2 c 3 a

Classwork/Groupwork suggestion
Practise the emphatic pronouns by chain drilling around the class/group. (To introduce some excitement, you could suggest that if anyone makes a mistake or hesitates too long, then the drill has to go back to the beginning and start again.) Use *did it* and the students cue the person, for example:
T: *I did it myself. They.*
S1: *They did it themselves. You.*
S2: *You did it yourself/yourselves. She.*
S3: *She did it herself. …*

Student's Book answers
4 1 cut yourself
   2 looking at herself
   3 waving to each other
   4 buy yourselves
   5 teaching myself
5 1 repaired it themselves
   2 it/one yourself
   3 did it myself
   4 painted it ourselves
   5 carry them yourselves
   6 open it itself
   7 cut it herself
   8 paid for it himself
6 1 myself 2 each other 3 itself 4 ourselves 5 yourselves
7 Answers will vary.

Pairwork suggestion
Elicit from the class and write on the board other things that students may or may not do themselves, e.g. cook breakfast, buy clothes.
In pairs, students ask and answer the questions, e.g. *Do you cook breakfast yourself?* They then report back to the class about their partner, e.g. *She cooks/doesn't cook breakfast herself*.

Student's Book answers

Puzzle
They should feed each other.

Worksheet
Use this activity before the preview to elicit/preteach new verbs *feed, pay, point, repair* and to revise other verbs in this unit.

Answers
1a wave, b point   2a break, b repair   3a buy, b pay
4a make, b do   5a cut, b cook   6a feed, b eat
7a open, b close

I really enjoyed myself

Worksheet 16

Complete the arrows under the verbs to match them with the pictures.

1a		wave ———— point ————>	b
2a		break ———— repair ————	b
3a		pay ———— buy ————	b
4a		do ———— make ————	b
5a		cook ———— cut ————	b
6a		feed ———— eat ————	b
7a		close ———— open ————	b

From GRAMMAR WORKS 2 by Mick Gammidge
© Cambridge University Press 1998

17 I used to forget everything!

Used to + infinitive; affirmative and negative forms

Meaning
Used to is used for regular actions or states in the past which were discontinued at a point in the past. It is often used for past habits.

Form
- In constructions with *used to* the main verb is in the infinitive.
- Draw students' attention to the difference in affirmative and negative forms: *used to/didn't use to*.

Pronunciation
The stress falls on *used/didn't use* and the main verb: *to* is an unstressed, weak form: /tə/.

Vocabulary
Verb: *used to*
Nouns: *basin, cave, ground, hot dog, mammoth, skin*
Adverbs: *clearly, on foot*

▶ Worksheet A

Preview activity
Ask students *Have you got a good memory? Do you remember things? What things do you often/sometimes forget? What do you do to help you remember things?*

Student's Book answers
1b 1 F 2 T 3 T 4 F
  c Studying used to be a problem – b
2a + I **used to** forget everything!
   – I **didn't use to** enjoy it.
   ? **Did** you **use to** enjoy school?
   What did you **use to** forget?
  b + Carol **used to** hate studying.
   – She **didn't use to** remember things.
   ? **Did** she **use to** forget names?
   What did she **use to** hate?
3 1 They used to sleep on the ground.
  2 They used to live in caves.
  3 They used to wear animal skins.
  4 They used to eat mammoths.
  5 They used to use stone tools.
  6 They used to travel on foot.
4 1 They didn't use to sleep in beds.
  2 They didn't use to live in houses.
  3 They didn't use to wear jeans.
  4 They didn't use to eat hamburgers.
  5 They didn't use to use computers.
  6 They didn't use to travel by aeroplane.

▶ Worksheet B

Groupwork suggestion
Students think of about five sentences with *used to / didn't use to* to describe their country/town in the past. If you wish, you could expand this activity into project work, where students research some facts about, for example, their town 100 years ago and produce an illustrated poster/album.

Student's Book answers
5 1 Did she use to sing beautifully? Yes, she did.
  2 Did she use to like writing? No, she didn't.
  3 Did she use to enjoy tennis? Yes, she did.
  4 Did she use to understand maths? No, she didn't.
  5 Did she use to remember places? No, she didn't.
6 1 didn't use to be 2 used to hate 3 Did she use to be 4 did she used to do 5 used to play 6 gave 7 was 8 used to wear

Extension activity
Students write sentences about what their families say they used to be like when they were little. Ask students to read interesting sentences to the class.

Student's Book answers
7 Answers will vary.

Puzzle
I used to forget everything – but now I ... I ... er...
I used to be a tap dancer – but then I fell in the basin.
I used to think that a hot dog – was a pet with a jumper on in summer.

Worksheet

A Use this activity before the preview to review verbs in exercise 1.

Answers
1 remember 2 forget 3 understand 4 know 5 think

B Use this activity after exercise 4 to review the new words in exercise 3.

Answers
1 caves 2 skins 3 ground 4 tools 5 mammoths

I used to forget everything!

Worksheet 17

A Complete the conversations with the verbs below.

forget   know   remember   think   understand

1. Where were you at 3.30 last Friday? — I'm sorry I can't _____ .
2. It's raining. — Oh, no! I always _____ my umbrella.
3. ✱✲✳✴✵✶✷✸✹✺✻ — I'm sorry. I don't _____ .
4. What's the biggest city in England? — I _____ ! It's London.
5. Whose is this? — I _____ that it's Sue's.

B Complete the sentences from this book about life 50,000 years ago. Use the words below.

caves   ground   mammoths   skins   tools

1. People used to live in _____ .
2. They used to wear _____ .
3. They used to sleep on the _____ .
4. They used to use stone _____ .
5. They used to hunt _____ .

18 I won't be able to live without you

Could/Couldn't
Will/Won't be able to

You may wish to use this as an opportunity to review *can* for ability.

Meaning
Here, *could* is used for ability in the past. *Will be able to* is used for ability in the future.
- Check that students' pronunciation isn't confused by the spelling; *l* is silent in *could*: /kʊd/.
- In *will be able to*, the stress falls on *able* and the main verb. *Be* and *to* are unstressed and *to* is pronounced /tə/.

Vocabulary
Nouns: *ability, building, plan, twins, vet*
Verbs: *be able to, could, rebuild, steal*

Student's Book answers
1 1b 2a 3c
2a + You **could smell** the Bad Brothers from 200 metres.
 – He **couldn't catch** them.
 ? Will he **be able to** walk?
 Yes, he **will**. He**'ll be able to** run.
 b *could* *will be able to*
 + He **could** do it. He**'ll be able to** do it.
 – He **couldn't** do it. He **won't be able to** do it.
 ? Could he do it? **Will** he **be able to** do it?
3 1 He'll be able to run fast.
 2 He won't be able to fly.
 3 He won't be able to swim.
 4 He'll be able to jump.
 5 He won't be able to save the plans.
 6 He'll be able to catch the Bad Brothers.

Groupwork suggestion
In small groups, students draw a diagram/picture of a different robotic animal of the future, e.g. a rabbit. Groups present their ideas to the class, e.g. *This is Roborabbit. She will be able to hear foxes at 50km. She will be able to jump 50m*, etc.

Student's Book answers
4 1 Will she be able to walk?
 2 Will she be able to see?
 3 Will she be able to hear?
 4 Will I be able to take her home?
5 1 He could make models.
 2 He couldn't paint pictures.
 3 He could use a computer.
 4 He couldn't play football.
 5 He could read.
 6 He couldn't ride a bicycle.
6 1 Could you make models?
 2 Could you paint pictures?
 3 Could you use a computer?
 4 Could you play football?
 5 Could you read?
 6 Could you ride a bicycle?

Pairwork suggestion
Students ask and answer their questions in pairs.

Student's Book answers
7 Answers will vary.

Puzzle

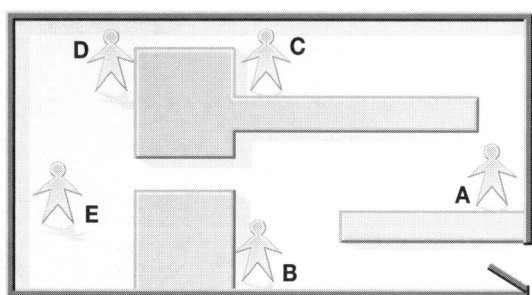

▶ Worksheet

Worksheet

Use this activity at the end of the unit to revise and consolidate basic verbs (many of which are used in the unit). The verbs are not given on the worksheet, so you may want to put students in groups to complete the worksheet or tell them that this is a memory test and set a time limit.

Answers
1 catch 2 dance 3 dive 4 draw 5 drive – a car 6 fly
7 hit 8 jump 9 kick 10 paint 11 play 12 read 13 ride
14 run 15 sing 16 smell 17 swim 18 throw 19 walk
20 write

I won't be able to live without you

Worksheet 18

Make a verb dictionary. Look at the pictures and write verbs for the actions.

1 _____	2 _____	3 _____	4 _____
5 _____	6 _____	7 _____	8 _____
9 _____	10 _____	11 _____	12 _____
13 _____	14 _____	15 _____	16 _____
17 _____	18 _____	19 _____	20 _____

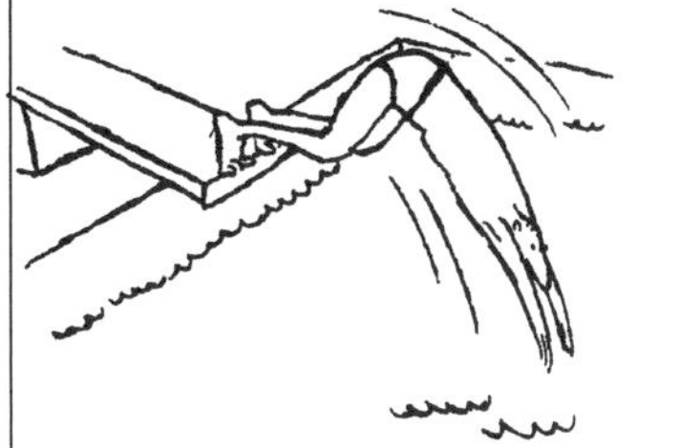

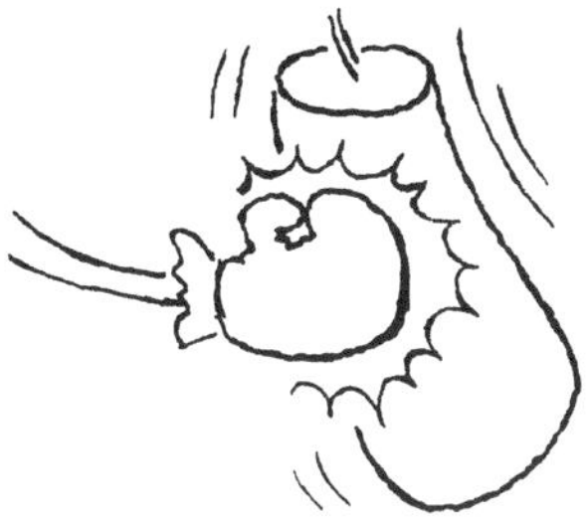

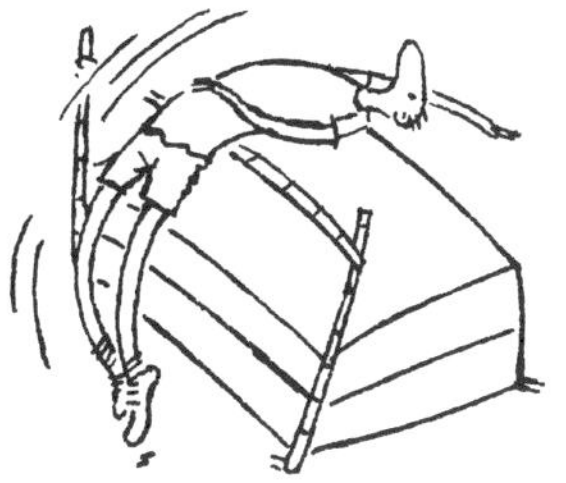

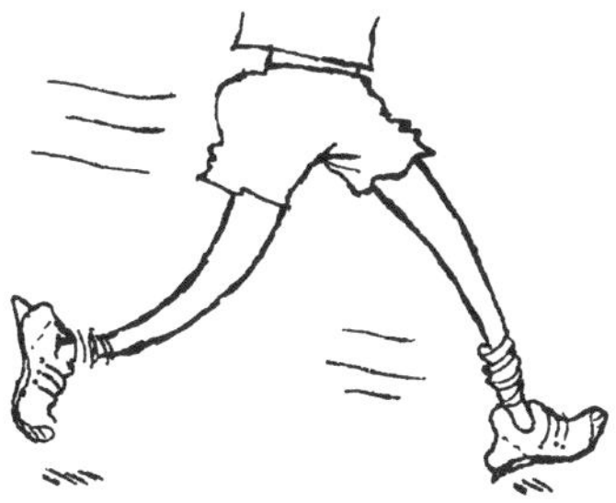

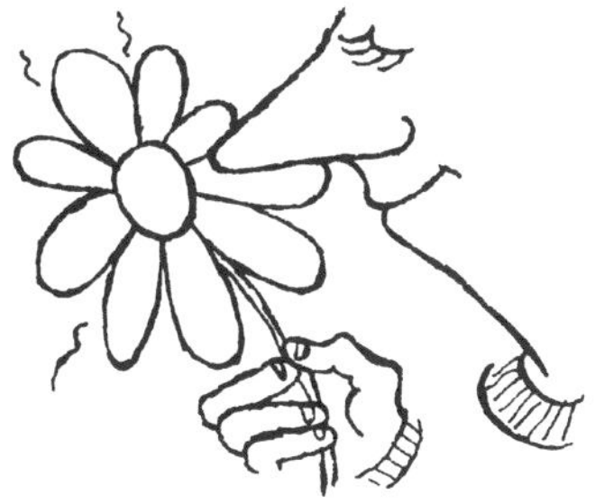

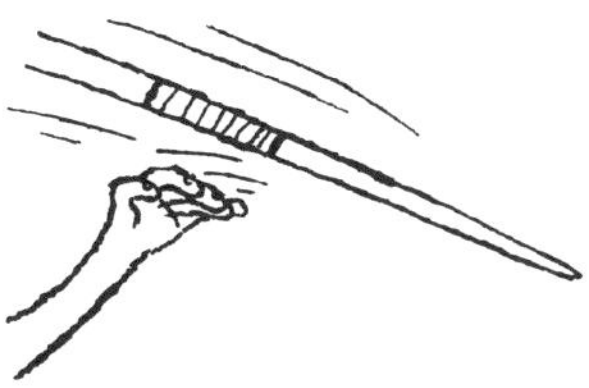

From GRAMMAR WORKS 2 by Mick Gammidge
© Cambridge University Press 1998

PHOTOCOPIABLE

Check point 13-18

1
1. What was he doing at 4 o'clock? He was looking at the paintings.
2. What was she doing at 4 o'clock? She was reading (a newspaper).
3. What were they doing at 4 o'clock? They were playing tennis.
4. What was he doing at 4 o'clock? He was sleeping.
5. What were they doing at 4 o'clock? They were arguing (with each other).
6. What were you doing at 4 o'clock?

2
1. He was feeding the dog when it bit him.
2. While she was carrying her shopping, she dropped the oranges.
3. While they were playing football, they broke the window.
4. She was cycling to school when an accident happened.

3
1. which sees
2. who invented
3. who (first) climbed
4. which flies
5. who (first) ran

4
1. It's washing itself.
2. I made it myself.
3. She can't repair it herself.
4. They're making their dinner themselves.
5. He heard himself on the radio.
6. They love each other.

5
1. she didn't use to exercise.
2. didn't use to watch
3. I didn't use to take
4. he used to play
5. she used to walk
6. we used to live

6
1. At 8 she'll be able to use a computer.
2. At 6 she won't be able to use a computer, but she will be able to write.
3. At 5 she won't be able to write, but she will be able to read.
4. At 3 she couldn't read, but she could talk.
5. At 2 she couldn't talk, but she could walk.
6. At 1 she couldn't walk, but she could crawl.

Double check! 13-18

1
1. Mr and Mrs Smith were eating dinner.
2. Tom was brushing his teeth.
3. Lucy was doing her homework.
4. Jim and Jane were watching TV.
5. Ian was washing his dog.
6. Val and Jenny were listening to the radio.

2
1. Which ones? / ones
2. Which one? / one
3. Which one? / one
4. Which ones? / ones

3
1. She didn't use to have a car.
2. She used to live in a small room.
3. She didn't use to wear expensive clothes.
4. She used to work every day.
5. She didn't use to eat in restaurants.

4
1. couldn't go
2. won't be able to play
3. couldn't draw
4. could read
5. 'll be able to cycle

Double check! 13–18

1 At 9.00 last night, someone turned off the electricity in the building.
Use the past continuous to write sentences about the people in the pictures.

1 Mr and Mrs Smith _were eating_ dinner.   **2** Tom _____ .   **3** Lucy _____ .

 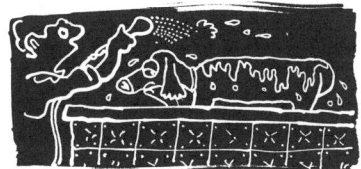 

4 Jim and Jane _____ .   **5** Ian _____ .   **6** Val and Jenny _____ .

---

2 Complete the conversations below with *Which ... ?* and *one/ones*.

1 A: Those shoes are mine.
   B: _Which ones_ ?
   A: The red _ones_ .

2 A: That boy is my brother.
   B: _____ ?
   A: The tallest _____ .

3 A: It's a clever cat.
   B: _____ ?
   A: The little black _____ .

4 A: Where are the magazines?
   B: _____ ?
   A: The new _____ .

3 This is Diane today. Look at the pictures of Diane five years ago and write sentences with *used to*.

1 _She didn't use to have_ a car.

2 _____ in a small room.

3 _____ expensive clothes.

4 _____ every day.

5 _____ in restaurants.

---

4 Complete the sentences with *could* or *'ll be able to* and the verbs below.

cycle   draw   ~~go~~   play   read

1 She was ill, so she _couldn't go_ to the party last night.

2 John _____ football tomorrow because he's got a broken leg.

3 The artists didn't have any pencils, so they _____ .

4 The professor was a clever girl. At two years old, she _____ books.

5 She's buying a bike, so she _____ to school.

From GRAMMAR WORKS 2 by Mick Gammidge
© Cambridge University Press 1998   PHOTOCOPIABLE

19 Smith asked her where the robot was

Direct and reported speech

Form

- In this introduction to reported speech, the grammar of *say*, *tell* and *ask* is contrasted:
  - We **say** something (to someone).
    He said that she could see.
  - We **tell** someone (about something/someone).
    He told them (that she could see).
  - We **ask** (someone) if/how/what/when/where/which/who/why …
    He asked (them) if she could see.
- After *say* and *tell*, *that* can be omitted.
- Direct speech is written inside speech marks, and the tense remains the same as the original speech.
- Reported speech does not use speech marks and the tense moves into the past. In this unit, present simple becomes past simple, present continuous becomes past continuous and *can* becomes *could*. (In modern English, this is beginning to change. Where the speech is still true in the present, e.g. *I can speak English*, then the tense often remains in the present when the speech is reported, e.g. *She said that she can speak English*.)

Vocabulary
Noun: *hospital*
Verb: *tell*
Conjunction: *if*

Student's Book answers
1b 1 ✓ 2 ✓ 3 ✗
2a 1 I can't tell you.
   2 She said that they were secret.
   3 The plans are for a robot.
   4 He/Smith said that he was looking for the plans.
b 1 said 2 told 3 told 4 said
3 1 Jones said that the robot was in his room.
   2 He told me that the robot was looking at him.
   3 He said that he could see Professor X.
   4 He told me that she was turning off the robot.

Classwork activity
Play 'Chinese Whispers'. Everybody sits in a circle. Whisper an interesting sentence to the student on your left, e.g. *The man with the black hat is taking the secret plans to my house*. The student reports the sentence to the student on his/her left, whispering, e.g. *She/He said / told me that the man in the black hat was taking the secret … *. The last student in the circle says the sentence to you out loud, e.g. *You said that the man … *. The idea is to see how close to the original sentence the last report is.

Student's Book answers
4 1 Where are the plans?
   2 I asked her if she knew Professor X.
   3 Where is the robot?
   4 Smith asked her if it was dangerous.

▶ Worksheet A

Student's Book answers
5 1 She asked me where I was going.
   2 He asked me if I wanted a drink.
   3 They asked her what she wanted.
   4 She asked them why they were asking.
   5 He asked him if he could play the piano.
   6 He asked her if he remembered the song.

Classwork activity
Prepare slips of paper with a different simple question or statement on each, e.g. *What time is it?*, *I am fifty years old*. Give a slip of paper to each student and tell them to read it to another student. They must remember the sentence they hear. When students have done this, they report back to the class, for example:
S1: *Juan asked me what time it was*.
S2: *Maria said that she was fifty years old*.

Student's Book answers
6 1 Sue asked where Kim was.
   2 Eric asked her if she could see her.
   3 She said that she couldn't see her anywhere.
   4 He said that he could see her.
   5 She asked him where she was.
   6 He said/told her that she was playing with the band.
7 Answers will vary.

▶ Worksheet B

Student's Book answers

Puzzle
The doctor is the boy's mother.

Worksheet

Extra vocabulary: *clarinet, flute, recorder, saxophone, trumpet, violin*

A Use this activity after exercise 4 to consolidate reporting verbs.

Answers
1 say 2 speak 3 Ask 4 tell 5 speak 6 say 7 Ask 8 Tell

B Use this activity after exercise 6 for vocabulary revision.

Answers
1 clarinet 2 drums 3 flute 4 guitar 5 piano 6 recorder 7 saxophone 8 trumpet 9 violin

Extension activity
Do a class survey. Students ask each other what instruments they can play. (You may need to help with extra vocabulary.) Collate the information. For a record, students can draw bar graphs and write up their findings using reported speech, e.g. *Four students said that they could play the piano.*

Smith asked her where the robot was — Worksheet 19

A Complete the sentences. Use the words below twice.

ask   say   speak   tell

1 They're boring. They never _____ anything interesting.
2 She can _____ Greek.
3 _____ me a question.
4 I'll _____ you the answer.
5 Please _____ English.
6 Please _____ it again.
7 _____ her if she knows the answer.
8 _____ me about your holiday.

B Make a picture dictionary of musical instruments. Write the names of the things below. (You can look at the words at the bottom of the page for help.)

1 _____clarinet_____

2 _____

3 _____

4 _____

5 _____

6 _____

7 _____

8 _____

9 _____

violin   piano   guitar   drums   recorder   flute   saxophone   clarinet   trumpet

From GRAMMAR WORKS 2 by Mick Gammidge
© Cambridge University Press 1998

20 You must come home at 10.30

Must and have to
Can for permission

Must and have to: Meaning
- *Must* and *have to* are used here for obligation, though this often blurs into necessity.
- *Must* and *have to* have very similar meanings and are often indistinguishable. (It has traditionally been taught that the difference lies in where the obligation comes from. If the obligation is internal to the speaker, *must* is used. Where obligation is from an external source, *have to* is used. For example, *I must see my teacher* – I want to ask her a question. *I have to see my teacher* – she's told me to come and see her. This distinction, however, is not generally reflected in everyday usage.)
- *Mustn't* and *don't have to* have very different meanings. *Mustn't* is used for prohibition. *Don't have to* is used for lack of obligation/necessity, not prohibition.

Form
- The infinitive is used with *must* and *have to*.
- Contractions in negative forms are usually used except in formal, written English.

Pronunciation
Must and *have to* are unstressed in neutral contexts but are frequently stressed for emphasis. The first *t* is silent in *mustn't*: /mʌsnt/ and the *to* in *have to* is an unstressed weak form: /tə/.

Can
Can for permission is contrasted with *can* for ability, which the students have already learnt. Both these uses of *can* have the same form and pronunciation.

Vocabulary
Nouns: *hamburger, library, permission*
Verbs: *have to, must, spend*

Preview activity
Ask students *What rules does your family have?* For example *Don't come home late*. Students compare the rules in their home with a partner. Ask for some examples from the class.

Student's Book answers
1b 1 yes 2 no 3 5 o'clock
2a 1 = ability 2 = permission
  b 1 no 2 no
  c 1 no 2 yes
3a 1 You **must** come home at 10.30.
   2 You **mustn't** be late.
   3 You **have to** get up early.
   4 They **don't have to** get up at 5 o'clock.
  b 1 You must get enough sleep.
   2 You mustn't come home at 12.00.
   3 You have to meet your granddad.
   4 They don't have to come home at 10.30.

Groupwork suggestion
In groups, students list as many school rules as they can, using *must/have to/mustn't*. Collate groups' rules on the board and check that everyone agrees what the rules are. You could then take a vote on whether students think each rule is a good one or a bad one.

Student's Book answers
4 1 Yes, you can. But you mustn't spend it on sweets.
   2 No, you can't. You must do your homework.
   3 No, you can't. You must be quiet. Your father is sleeping.
   4 Yes, you can. But you must finish your homework first.
   5 No, you can't. You mustn't eat junk food.
5 1 She has to go to school.
   2 She has to stay in bed.
   3 He doesn't have to pay.
   4 They don't have to walk to school.
   5 You have to wait at the traffic lights.
   6 She doesn't have to get up early.

Pairwork suggestion
With a partner, students write as many ideas they can beginning *On Sunday*, and using *have to / don't have to*. Students read their best ideas to the class.

Student's Book answers
6 1 I mustn't be late.
   2 The café doesn't open on Sunday afternoons, so I don't have to work.
   3 I have to wear a white shirt.
   4 I mustn't drop the plates.
   5 I have to be careful in the kitchen.
   6 I have to speak politely all the time!

▶ Worksheet
Student's Book answers
7 Answers will vary.

Puzzle
At 60kmh, 30 km takes 30 minutes. The motorway, 15 km, takes 15 minutes, but there is also 10 minutes waiting making it 25 minutes. So the motorway is still faster.

Worksheet

Extra vocabulary: *fork*

Use this activity after exercise 6 for vocabulary revision. (You may want to put students in groups and/or set a time limit and have a competition to complete this worksheet.)

Answers
1 window 2 door 3 mirror 4 painting 5 board 6 money
7 bottle 8 dish 9 knife 10 glass 11 fork 12 salt
13 pepper 14 spoon 15 cup 16 plate 17 table 18 chair
19 box 20 phone

You must come home at 10.30

Worksheet

Look at the picture of the café. How many things can you name?

10 = good
15 = very good
20 = excellent!

1 _____	2 _____	3 _____	4 _____	5 _____
6 _____	7 _____	8 _____	9 _____	10 _____
11 _____	12 _____	13 _____	14 _____	15 _____
16 _____	17 _____	18 _____	19 _____	20 _____

From **GRAMMAR WORKS 2** by Mick Gammidge
© Cambridge University Press 1998

PHOTOCOPIABLE

21 The work has been hard

Present perfect simple with *just, already, yet*

Meaning
- The present perfect simple has many meanings in English, but here it is used for completed past actions where the focus is on their consequence/result in the present. For example:
  – *I've lost my keys* – I can't open the door now.
  – *I lost my keys* – but it's not a problem now; I found/replaced them.
- *Just* is used to emphasise that an event/action is extremely recent.
- *Already* is used when it is necessary to emphasise that an action/event is completed before now.
- *Yet* is used in negatives and generally emphasises that an event/action hasn't happened but we expect that it will.
- In the present perfect simple, *be* can mean *visit*, but this meaning also contrasts with that of *go*. For example:
  – *She has been to America* = She has visited America and returned;
  – *She has gone to America* = She has not returned.

Form
- The present perfect simple is formed with the present simple of *have* as an auxiliary verb and the past participle of the main verb.
- The auxiliary is generally contracted in spoken English (though full forms can be used for emphasis), and full forms are generally used in written English.
- The past participle form for regular verbs is the same as the past simple, but irregular past simple forms also have irregular past participles. Drilling from the infinitive to the past form to the past participle is useful practice in learning these.
- *Just* and *already* are usually placed between *have* and the main verb; *yet* is usually placed after the object or objects of the verb.

Pronunciation
- Contractions are usually used, but when full forms are used, e.g. in formal situations, these are normally unstressed weak forms: /həv/, /həz/ or /əv/, /əz/.
- The strong forms /hæv/, /hæz/ are only used for emphasis.

Vocabulary
Nouns: *bead, villager, well*
Adverbs: *already, just, yet*

Preview activity
Ask *Why is water important for us? What do we use it for? Where does it come from?*

▶ **Worksheet**

Student's Book answers
1b 1 five 2 no 3 no
  2
infinitive	past simple	past participle
be	was/were	been
build	built	built
do	did	done
give	gave	given
see	saw	seen
start	started	started
take	took	taken

3a + The villagers **have done** the work.
  + The work **has been** hard.
  – The people **haven't built** a well.
  b + The people in Anoma's village **have built** a well.
  – The work **hasn't been** easy.

4 1 They have built the school.
  2 They have painted the school.
  3 They haven't made the tables and chairs.
  4 She hasn't bought the books.
  5 She has spoken to the parents.
  6 She has met the students.
5a 1 b 2 c 3 a
  b 1 b 2 c 3 a
6 1 He's just hit his thumb.
  2 He's just taken a photo.
  3 They've just seen a film.
  4 She's already finished.
  5 He hasn't woken up yet.
  6 She's already written three letters.

Groupwork activity
Students stand/sit in a circle and take it in turns to mime/do a quick action, e.g. drop a pen, cough, clap, etc. The student on the performer's left says *You've just dropped your pen*, etc. then performs their own action, and so on around the circle. If a student can't provide the answer, the other students in the group can help.

Student's Book answers
7 Answers will vary. Suggestions:
  I have just finished exercise 6.
  I haven't finished exercise 7 yet.
  I have already done exercise 5, etc.

Personalisation activity
Write a list of things on the board which includes things that you know your students have done already and things that they haven't done yet, e.g. get a job, learn to drive, have breakfast, learn the present simple in English, etc. Students write sentences about themselves using the present perfect and *already* and *yet*.

Student's Book answers

Puzzle

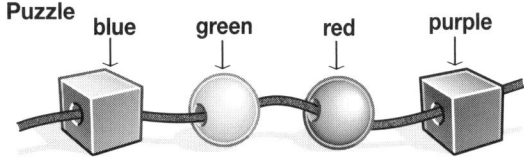

blue green red purple

Worksheet

Extra vocabulary: *evaporation, lake*

Use this activity after the preview activity and before exercise 1 to preteach *well*.

Answers
1 evaporation 2 sun 3 cloud 4 wind 5 mountain 6 rain
7 snow 8 river 9 lake 10 sea 11 well 12 tap
13 drinking water

The work has been hard

Worksheet 21

Look at the diagram about water. Write the words below with the things in the diagram.

cloud   drinking water   ~~evaporation~~   lake   mountain   rain   river   sea   snow   sun   tap   well   wind

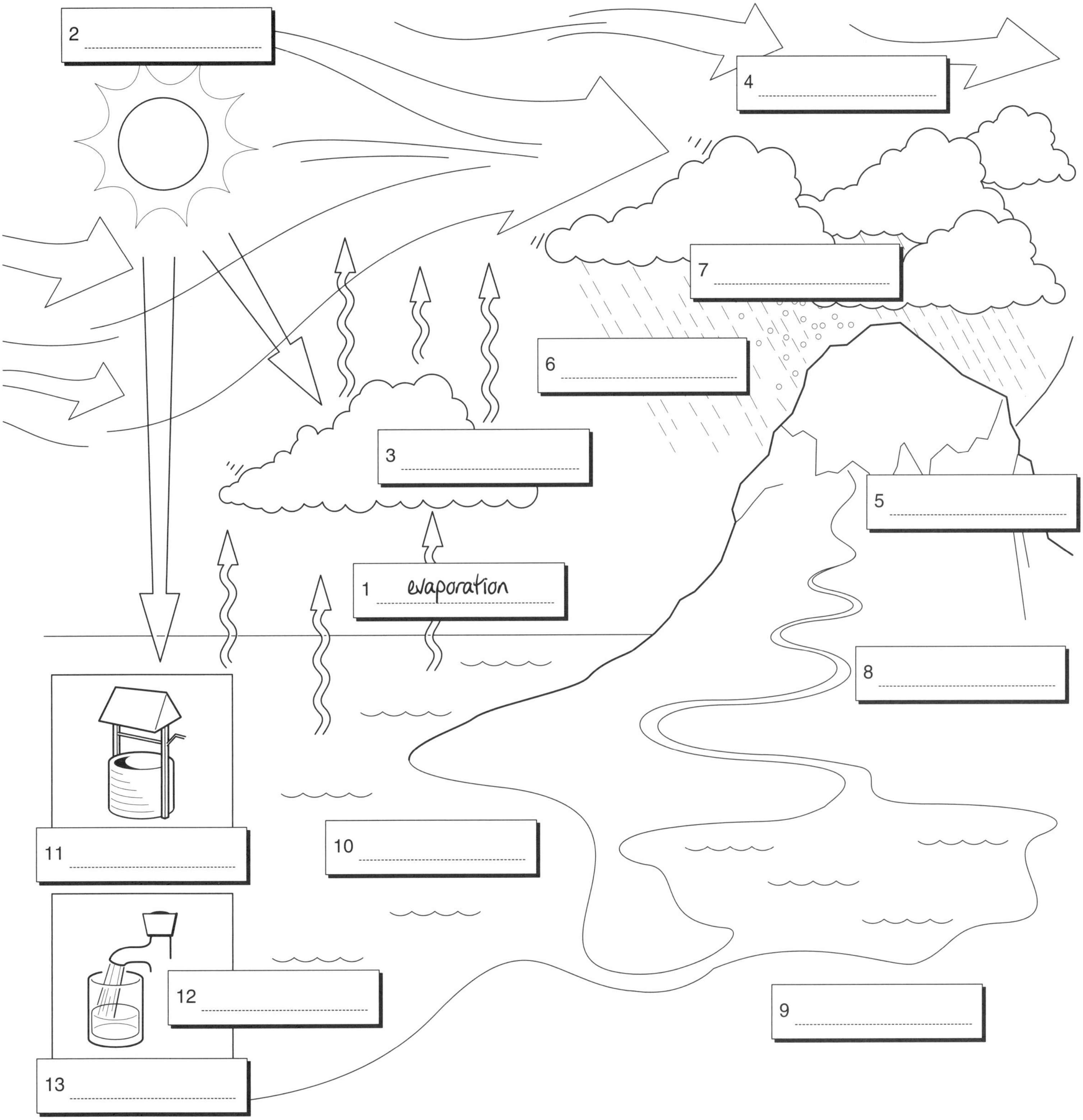

1. evaporation
2. ___
3. ___
4. ___
5. ___
6. ___
7. ___
8. ___
9. ___
10. ___
11. ___
12. ___
13. ___

From GRAMMAR WORKS 2 by Mick Gammidge
© Cambridge University Press 1998

PHOTOCOPIABLE

22 Where have you put the chocolates?

Present perfect simple, question forms with *ever* ... ?

Form
Questions in the present perfect simple are made by putting the auxiliary before the subject. *Wh-* question words are placed before the auxiliary.

Meaning
- In present perfect simple questions, *ever* is used to mean 'on any occasion' or 'at any time' and is often used in questions about life experience.
- *When* questions about specific time points generally use the past simple rather than the present perfect.

Vocabulary
Nouns: *chocolate, France, shape*
Verb: *ski*
Adverb: *ever*

Preview activity
Elicit all the names of countries/continents that students can remember and write them on the board. Review pronunciation and spelling.

▶ *Worksheet*

Student's Book answers
1 1 T   2 T   3 F
2a 1 Have you finished your homework?
    2 Yes, I have.
    3 Where have you put the chocolates?
 b 1 **Have** Elena and Kim **finished** their homework?
    1 Yes, **they have**.
    2 **Who has eaten** the chocolates?
      Liam has!
3 1 **Have** we **arrived** early?
    2 **Have** you **used** pepper?
    3 What **have** you **cooked**?
    4 **Have** your parents **gone out**?
    5 Who **has eaten** the chocolates?
4a 1 ever 2 never
 b 1 ever 2 never
 c 1 a 2 b
5 1 Have you ever eaten fish and chips?   No, I haven't.
    2 Have you ever ridden a donkey?   No, I haven't.
    3 Have you ever swum in the sea?   Yes, I have.
    4 Have you ever stayed in a hotel?   No, I haven't.
    5 Have you ever played tennis?   Yes, I have.

Pairwork suggestion
In pairs, students ask each other the questions in exercise 5 and give their own true, expanded answers.

Student's Book answers
6 1 've broken   2 Have you <u>ever</u> broken   3 bought
    4 have <u>never</u> been   5 I've watched   6 Have (you) paid (for the holiday) <u>yet</u>   7 went   8 hasn't planned (her holiday) <u>yet</u>
7 Answers will vary.

Classwork activity
Play 'Find someone who ...'. Students ask others the questions in exercise 7. They aim to find someone in the class who has/hasn't done the same things that they have. When students have found a partner, they sit down.

Student's Book answers

Puzzle
Shape c.

Worksheet

Use these activities after the preview activity and before exercise 1. Use activity B to preteach *chocolate*.
Extra vocabulary: *Germany, Norway, India, Mexico*

A Answers
1 Mexico   2 Caribbean   3 Norway   4 Germany   5 France
6 Spain   7 Italy   8 Greece   9 Africa   10 Turkey
11 India   12 China

Extension activity
In pairs/groups, students put the names of the places from the board (see the preview activity) on the map.

B Answers
1 chocolate, tomato   2 potato   3 skis   4 hamburger
5 café, restaurant   6 mosquito   7 piano, umbrella
8 geography, science   9 banana   10 coffee   11 shampoo
12 tea

Extension activity
After exercise 6, return to the worksheet. Students write questions using the present perfect and the places and things from the worksheet, e.g. *Have you ever drunk coffee in Turkey? Has your mother ever played the piano in Italy?*

Where have you put the chocolates? Worksheet 22

A Look at the map and write the names of the places 1–12.

Africa   Caribbean   China   France   Germany   Greece   India   Italy   ~~Mexico~~   Norway   Spain   Turkey

B The English names of the things in the pictures come from the languages of places 1–12. Write the English names of the things.

1 Mexico
   chocolate

2 _____

3 _____

4 _____

12 _____

5 _____

11 _____

6 _____

10 _____   9 _____   8 _____   7 _____

C Do you know any English words which come from your language?

23 If he isn't fit, he won't play in the big match

First conditional

Meaning
The first conditional is used to talk about futures which are clearly possible. The *if* clause describes the possible event which needs to happen before the event in the other clause can happen. Both refer to future, despite their different tenses.

Form
- The *if* clause uses the present simple and the conditional clause uses the future simple.
- Where the *if* clause begins a sentence, it is followed by a comma.

Vocabulary
Nouns: *exam, final, player, semi-final, team, trophy*
Verb: *pass (exam)*
Adverb: *on time*

▶ **Worksheet**

Student's Book answers
1b 1 yes 2 don't know 3 no 4 don't know
2a 1 They'll play Chelsea **if** they win.
2 **If** he isn't fit**,** he won't play.
b 1 Derby **will** keep the trophy **if** they win the final.
2 **If** Stoke win tomorrow, they**'ll play** Chelsea next week.
3 **If** Stoke don't win tomorrow, they **won't play** Chelsea next week.
c future
3 1 f 2 c 3 e 4 a 5 b 6 d
4 1 If she doesn't work hard, she won't pass her exams.
2 If he drives dangerously, he'll have an accident.
3 If you don't take exercise, you won't get fit.
4 If they don't get up, they'll be late for school.
5 If he forgets his umbrella, he'll get wet.
6 If she doesn't do her homework, her teacher will be angry.

Classwork activity
Each student writes their own first conditional sentence, putting each clause on a separate piece of paper. They put all the *if* clauses in one bag and all the *will* clauses in another bag. Each student then pulls out a slip from each bag without looking. Students then try to match up the clauses to make sentences by milling around the classroom. One student reads out their *if* clause to another student, who reads out their *will* clause. If the *will* clause matches, the first student can take the paper. The other student then reads out their *if* clause and the first student replies with their *will* clause. Students keep going from partner to partner until they have matched both clauses. They then sit down. Monitor for pronunciation. (Students sometimes tend to simply look at each other's slips. To avoid this, you can have the students memorise their slips before starting and put them in their pockets.)

Student's Book answers
5 1 If James comes home late, his mum will be angry.
2 If his mum is angry, she won't cook him any dinner.
3 If she doesn't cook him dinner, he'll be hungry.
4 If he is hungry, he won't sleep well.
5 If he doesn't sleep well, he won't wake up on time.
6 If he doesn't wake up on time, he'll be late for school.
7 If he is late for school, his mum will be angry.

Pairwork activity
Students play 'First conditional tennis' with their partner. The first student gives an *if* clause and the second student finishes the sentence with an appropriate *will* clause. He/She then provides the next *if* clause which is a transformation of the *will* clause from the sentence they have just finished. The first student completes the sentence and forms the next *if* clause in the same way. Students keep going until one student is unable to think of a completion. The game is then over. (Students can play the best of three games.) For example:
S1: *If it's sunny at the weekend,*
S2: *I'll go to the beach. If I go to the beach,*
S1: *I'll buy an ice cream. If I buy an ice-cream,*
S2: *I'll eat it. If I eat it,*
S1: *I'll get fat. If I get fat, etc.*

Student's Book answers
6 1 If she doesn't find her dog, she'll cry.
2 If he drops the plates, they'll break.
3 The cat will bite her if she doesn't feed it.
4 He will phone the police if she doesn't pay.
5 They will chase her if she turns off the TV.
6 If they don't wake up, they won't catch any fish.
7 Answers will vary.

Puzzle
Sally has got 24 sweets.

Worksheet

Use these activities as a preview activity before exercise 1 to preteach *final, player, semi-final, team, trophy*.

Answers
A 1 art, artist 2 farm, farmer 3 music, musician
4 paint, painter 5 science, scientist 6 cook, cook
7 drive, driver 8 fish, fisherman 9 play, player
10 work, worker

Answers
B 1 match 2 stadium 3 goal 4 team 5 trophy
6 semi-final 7 final

If he isn't fit, he won't play in the big match — Worksheet 23

A Complete the charts.

noun (thing)	person	verb	person
1 art	artist	6 cook	
2 farm		7 drive	
3 music		8 fish	
4 paint		9 play	
5 science		10 work	

B Look at the sports page from a newspaper. Put the words below in the correct places.

final   goal   ~~match~~   semi final   stadium   team   trophy

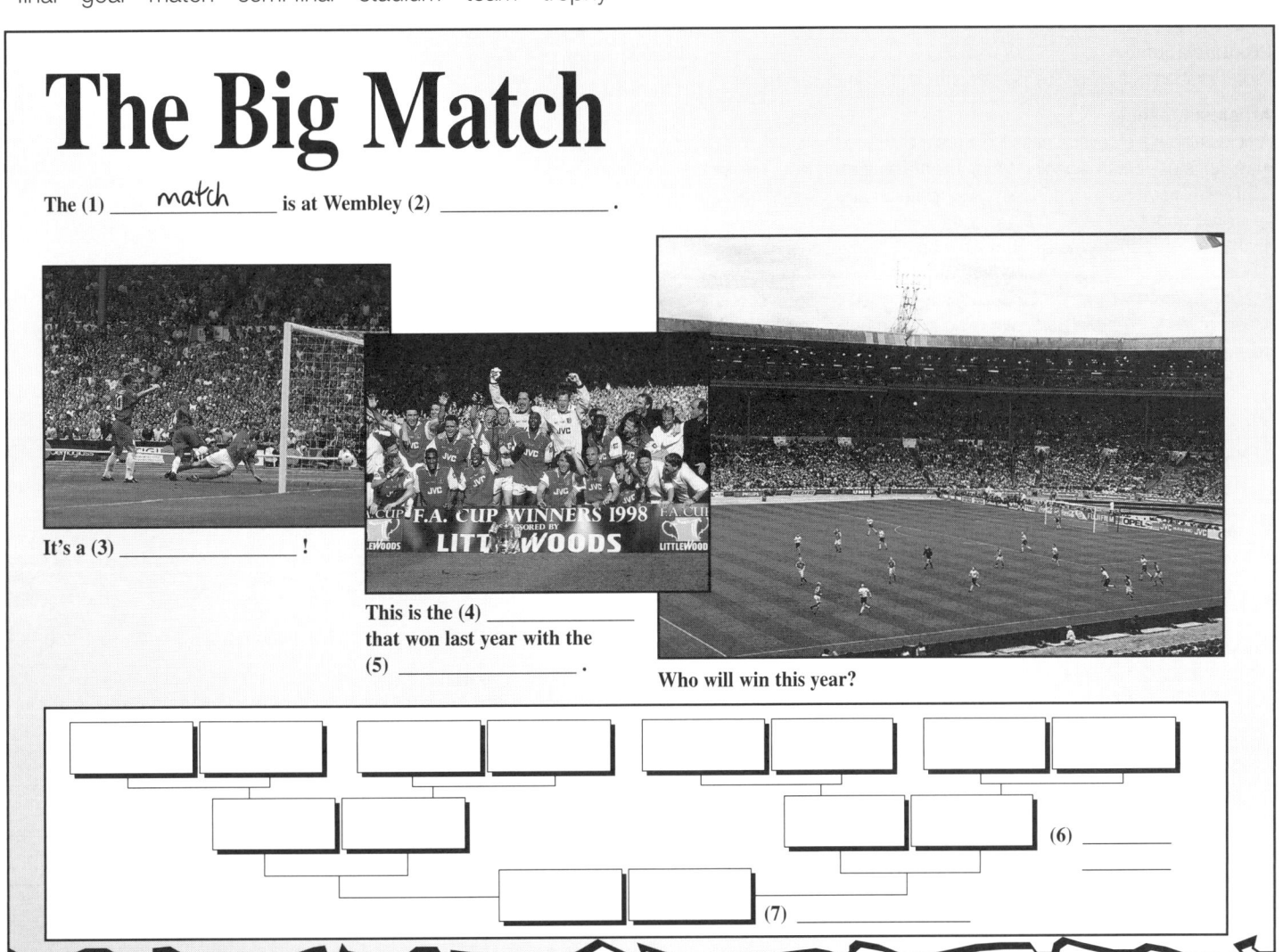

The Big Match

The (1) __match__ is at Wembley (2) _____ .

It's a (3) _____ !

This is the (4) _____ that won last year with the (5) _____ .

Who will win this year?

(6) _____

(7) _____

From GRAMMAR WORKS 2 by Mick Gammidge
© Cambridge University Press 1998

24 Honey is eaten everywhere

The passive past and present (affirmative forms)
Articles

The passive: Meaning
- The passive has several uses in English, but here it is used for situations where:
  - we don't know who does/did the action. For example:
    My bag was stolen. = someone stole my bag. (I don't know who.)
  - the action, or the person/thing it happens to, is more interesting/important than the person/thing who does it. For example:
    Bees are kept by farmers.
    The queen was bitten by a dog.
- *By* is used to talk about the person/thing that does/did the action.

Form
- The passive is formed by using *be* as an auxiliary, in the appropriate tense, and the past participle of the main verb. The subject and object exchange places when an active sentence is put into the passive, and *by* is used to show the agent (doer) of the action. For example:
  Farmers keep bees.
  Bees are kept by farmers.
- When the agent is unknown or unimportant it can be omitted.

Pronunciation
Pronunciation of auxiliary *be* is the same as in continuous tenses.

Articles: Meaning
Articles also have several uses in English, but here:
- *A/An* is used with singular countable nouns for the first time, when the listener/reader doesn't know which particular thing is being talked about.
- *The* is used about the same noun when it is mentioned again because that particular thing is now known by the listener/reader.
- *The* is also used when something is mentioned for the first time if everyone knows the particular thing being mentioned.

Pronunciation
- Articles are usually unstressed weak forms.
- *A* and *an* are usually pronounced /ə/ and /ən/. (The pronunciations /eɪ/ and /æn/ are occasionally used for emphasis.)
- *The* is usually pronounced /ðə/, except before vowel sounds or for emphasis when it is pronounced /ðiː/.

Vocabulary
Nouns: bee, drone, flower, hive, honey, king, pyramid, queen, type

▶ Worksheet

Preview activity
Ask students *Do you like honey? When/How do you eat it? Where does it come from? Which animal makes it?*

Student's Book answers
1b 1 the workers 2 the workers 3 Karl von Frisch
2a 1 Honey Bees **are kept** by farmers.
   2 Honey **is made** by the worker bees.
   3 Their dance **was written** about by Karl von Frisch.
b 1 The drones **are chased** by the workers.
   2 The work **is done** by the workers.
   3 Bees **were studied** by Karl von Frisch.

3 1 Honey **is made** in a hive.
   2 Tea **is grown** in India.
   3 Orange juice **is drunk** in most countries.
   4 Chips **are cooked** in oil.
   5 Vegetables **are sold** in supermarkets.
   6 Dry grass **is fed** to horses.
   7 Sheep's eyes **are eaten** in some countries.
4 1 Pictures are painted by artists.
   2 The Mona Lisa was painted by Leonardo.
   3 Pyramids were built by the ancient Egyptians.
   4 They are visited by millions of people every year.
   5 The planets are studied by scientists.
   6 The telescope was invented by Galileo.
   7 Rice is grown by the Japanese.
   8 Rice is eaten by people everywhere.

Groupwork activity
In groups, students write five general knowledge questions, e.g. *Who wrote about the Bee Dance? Who invented the telephone?* They exchange their questions with another group. Groups write answers to the question, e.g. *Von Frisch wrote about the Bee Dance.* Groups get points for the right answer and points for correct grammar.

Student's Book answers
5a 1 They do **a** dance. **The** dance tells the other workers where to look.
   2 They live together in **a** hive. **The** hive is built by the workers.
b 1 Every hive has got **a** queen. **The** queen is fed by the workers.
   2 Karl von Frisch wrote **a** book. **The** book is about bees.
6 1 bought, a 2 was taken, The 3 was built, a 4 was called
   5 were kept, the 6 was given 7 went, the 8 went
   9 loved, a 10 flew 11 ran 12 was chased, the 13 saw
   14 fell 15 asked
7 Answers will vary.

Puzzle
Three babies (triplets) were born at the same time to the same parents!

Worksheet

Extra vocabulary: *X-ray*

Use this activity to preteach *bee, flower, honey, king, pyramid, queen* before the preview activity.

Answers
astronaut, bee, castle, dinosaur, Earth, flower, giraffe, honey, ice cream, jumper, king, lift, moon, nose, owl, pyramid, queen, rabbit, sock, trousers, umbrella, village, wheel, X-ray, year, zoo

Extension activity
In small groups, students write the alphabet, then take it in turns to choose a letter and give a word beginning with that letter. The letter is then crossed off the sheet. The next student then chooses another letter and gives the word for that letter which is then crossed off. If a student can't give a word, they are out of the game and the next student takes a turn. The winner is the last student left in the group.

Honey is eaten everywhere

Worksheet 24

Write a word for each letter of the alphabet.

Aa _____	Nn _____
Bb _____	Oo _____
Cc _____	Pp _____
Dd _____	Qq _____
Ee _____	Rr _____
Ff _____	Ss _____
Gg _____	Tt _____
Hh _____	Uu _____
Ii _____	Vv _____
Jj _____	Ww _____
Kk _____	Xx X-ray
Ll _____	Yy _____
Mm _____	Zz _____

From GRAMMAR WORKS 2 by Mick Gammidge
© Cambridge University Press 1998

Check point 19-24

1
1. She told me that the answer was easy.
2. He said that he couldn't hear me/us.
3. She asked me where I lived.
4. They said that they were twins.
5. We asked them what their names were.
6. She said that she could speak Spanish.
7. He told me that I was in the wrong class.

2a
1. You mustn't eat.
2. You mustn't talk loudly.
3. You mustn't play games.
4. You must leave at 5 pm.
5. You must bring books back in two weeks.
6. You mustn't take newspapers away.
7. You must bring your library card.

b
1. You don't have to bring books back in one week.
2. You mustn't eat.
3. You don't have to leave at 3 pm.

3
1a. Flash has already finished.
 b. Silver has just finished.
 c. Merlin hasn't finished yet.
2a. He has just woken up.
 b. She has already woken up.
 c. They haven't woken up yet.
3a. They haven't eaten yet.
 b. She has just eaten.
 c. He has already eaten.

4a
1. Have you ever eaten sheep's eyes?
2. Have you ever swum in the river Nile?
3. Have you ever been to South America?
4. Have you ever climbed Everest?
5. Have you ever ridden an elephant?

b
1. Yes, she has.
2. No, she hasn't.
3. No, she hasn't.
4. Yes, she has.
5. Yes, she has.

5a
1. eat too many burgers — get fat
2. not tidy room — not find her shoes
3. read newspapers — learn about the world
4. study hard — pass the exam
5. take too many books — not read them
6. wear a jumper — not get cold

b
1. If he eats too many burgers, he'll get fat.
2. If she doesn't tidy her room, she won't find her shoes.
3. If they don't read newspapers, they won't learn about the world.
4. If she doesn't study hard, she won't pass the exam.
5. If he takes too many books, he won't read them.
6. If she wears a jumper, she won't get cold.

6
1. built, was painted
2. are made, use
3. stole, were caught
4. is grown, drink
5. is completed. Can (you) speak

Double check! 19-24

1
1. You mustn't take photos.
2. You must turn left.
3. You mustn't drop litter.
4. You mustn't feed the elephants.
5. You mustn't drink the water.
6. You must wash your hands.

2
1. James asked his mum if she could wash his shirt.
2. Linda told Eric that she was coming home at 6.00.
3. James's mum told him that she couldn't because she was busy.
4. Eric asked Mark and Linda where his camera was.

3
1. They've been to Egypt.
2. He's (just) dropped his money.
3. The bus hasn't arrived (yet).
4. The pilot hasn't washed (yet).
5. She's broken her arm.

4
1. First, two glasses of carrot juice and one glass of pineapple juice are put in a jug.
2. Next, one lemon is squeezed.
3. The lemon juice is added to the jug.
4. Then the juice is poured into small glasses.
5. Finally, ice is added. It is stirred well.

Double check! 19–24

1 What do these signs mean? Write sentences with *You must/mustn't*.

1 _____
2 _____
3 _____
4 _____
5 _____
6 _____

2 Read the notes and write them with reported speech.

1
Mum
Can you wash my shirt?
James

2
Eric
I'm coming home at 6.00.
Linda

3
James
I can't because I'm busy.
Mum

4
Mark and Linda
Where's my camera?
Eric

1 James asked his mum if she could wash his shirt.

2 _____
3 _____
4 _____

3 Complete the sentences about the people in the picture. Use the present perfect and the verbs below.

arrive be break drop wash

1 They _____ Egypt.
2 He _____ his money.
3 The bus _____ .
4 The pilot _____ .
5 She _____ her arm.

4 Read the recipe for Cool Caribbean Carrot juice. Write the sentences in the passive.

1. First, put two glasses of carrot juice and one glass of pineapple juice in a jug.
2. Next, squeeze one lemon.
3. Add the lemon juice to the jug.
4. Then pour the juice into small glasses.
5. Finally, add ice. Stir it well.

1 First, two glasses of carrot juice and one glass of pineapple juice are put in a jug.

2 _____
3 _____
4 _____
5 _____